"This is one of the best books I have read on parenting an adult child. Sometimes it is incredibly complicated to deal with the complex issues of this particular season of our parenting journey. Nancy coaches us on all the important topics and brings us very practical advice. If you are trying to figure out this most fascinating time in the life of your family, like my wife and I are doing right now, read this book!"

Jim Burns, President, HomeWord
Author, *Teenology: The Art of Raising Great Teenagers*

"As I read through Nancy Williams's wonderful book *Secrets to Parenting Your Adult Child,* I found myself stopping every few pages as I'd stumble across yet another nugget of truth. Staring at her words, I'd say, 'Wow, if I would just do *that,* it would change everything!' As the mother of four grown daughters, I need all of the 'doable' advice I can get. I heartily recommend this book to parents of grown children. You will refer to it often!"

Janice Hanna Thompson,
Author, *The House Is Quiet, Now What?*

"For all of us who read the how-to parenting books when our children were young, here's an excellent resource now that our children are grown. *Secrets to Parenting Your Adult Child* offers valuable wisdom for the changes and challenges we face and provides the tools needed for strengthening these precious relationships."

Georgia Shaffer, PA Licensed Psychologist
Author, *Taking Out Your Emotional Trash*

"*Inspiring. Encouraging. Challenging.* These words describe Nancy Williams's thought-provoking book *Secrets to Parenting Your Adult Child.* As the mother of four adult children, I find the process of 'letting go' difficult. This book opened my eyes to the importance of setting them free. This book is a must for all parents!"

Carla McDougal, Reflective Life Ministries,
Author, *Reflecting Him: Living for Jesus and Loving It!*

Secrets to Parenting

your adult child

Nancy Williams

BETHANYHOUSE

MINNEAPOLIS, MINNESOTA

Published by Bethany House Publishers
11400 Hampshire Avenue South
Bloomington, Minnesota 55438

Bethany House Publishers is a division of
Baker Publishing Group, Grand Rapids, Michigan.

Printed in the United States of America

In keeping with biblical principles of creation stewardship, Baker Publishing Group advocates the responsible use of our natural resources. As a member of the Green Press Initiative, our company uses recycled paper when possible. The text paper of this book is comprised of 30% post-consumer waste.

green press INITIATIVE

Library of Congress Cataloging-in-Publication Data

Williams, Nancy.
    Secrets to parenting your adult child / Nancy Williams.
        p. cm.
    Includes bibliographical references.
    Summary: "Professional counselor and mom helps parents navigate the changing rela-
tionships with their adult children"—Provided by publisher.
    ISBN 978-0-7642-0855-3 (pbk. : alk. paper) 1. Parent and adult child. 2. Adult
children—Family relationships. 3. Intergenerational relations. I. Title.
    HQ755.86.W55   2011
    248.8'45—dc22
                                                            2010041178

Dedication

To Solon, whose love, wisdom, strength, partnership,
encouragement, and sense of humor bring joy
to our parenting journey.

And to Aaron, Andrea, Adam, and Eliza,
whose love, laughter, and support light up my life.

Acknowledgments

When I gave birth to my children, I wondered how I could be all they needed me to be and do all I wanted to do for them as a parent. To teach and guide, to love and protect, to encourage and prepare them to experience all God designed for their lives. I quickly realized I would not be alone on that journey. God blessed me with a wonderful husband along with family members and friends who continually grace me with their love, wisdom, laughter, and encouragement on this parenting journey. May He touch their lives with a special portion of His love and blessing.

God has been faithful so many times in my life to surround me with gifted, supportive people, and He has done so in great measure with the preparation of this book. Thank you to Janet Grant of Books & Such Literary Agency and Andy McGuire, Ellen Chalifoux, and the team at Bethany House for sharing the vision and partnering with me to offer these words of insight and encouragement to parents. I'm also blessed to have had a group of friends—*balcony people*—come alongside this book since its beginning with their prayers, contributions, and encouraging words, including Sharen Watson and Janice Hanna Thompson, who also shared their editorial skills along the way.

This book is filled with stories from parents who are traveling this journey along with me. I am grateful they have candidly shared from their own parenting experiences to encourage others traveling this same path. Names and some details have been changed to protect the privacy of their families, but God knows who they are. And I pray He will bless them for the love offering they have given from their hearts. I'm also thankful to those professionals who have offered words of insight and instruction. May God bless the work they are doing to help others find hope and healing, and experience life to the fullest.

Contents

Just When You Thought Your Work Was Done . . .

"The hardest part of raising a child is teaching them to ride bicycles. A shaky child on a bicycle for the first time needs both support and freedom. The realization that this is what the child will always need, can hit hard."
—SLOAN WILSON, NOVELIST

I held my little one in my arms, and my husband set the suitcase down and curled up next to us on the bed as we shared our first few moments at home together as a family. We couldn't stop smiling as we looked at that innocent, perfectly formed little person and then into each other's eyes. We had a new identity.

"Hi, Mom."

"Hi, Dad."

While our son lay there quietly, nestled among the pillows and surrounded by his proud parents, we dreamed about the future that was ahead for our new little family. Our thoughts bounced back and forth from excitement to fear, from confidence to uncertainty. We vowed to do our best as caregivers, protectors, guides, providers, defenders, and teachers. Parents.

"Can we really do this? Are we ready?" I wondered if I could measure up to all the books I had read and examples I had seen about how to be a great mother. My husband gently took my hand and offered assurance: "Nancy, we'll be fine. God gave him to us, and if we stay close together and listen to Him, He'll help us be the best parents we can be."

Sound familiar? If you are a parent of grown children like us, you probably had that same experience as you took on the role of raising a child. When we all cradled our newborns in our arms those many years ago, we envisioned spending eighteen years or so training our children in the way they should go and then launching them off into adulthood. We assumed we would complete our parental tasks and face the "empty nest."

The pages on the calendar seemed to turn quickly, and before we knew it we watched our children blow out eighteen candles on a birthday cake. As we celebrated this milestone in their lives, our minds drifted back to our own graduation from teenager to adult. For many of us, the ink was barely dry on our diploma when we heard the good-byes and well-wishes from family and friends. Some with tear-filled eyes and others with sighs of relief. Armed with a set of luggage, the old family car, warnings from Dad, and a care package from Mom, we headed out the door and into our future.

Whatever the circumstances, whether off to college, away to the military, or out to find a job and our own apartment, we left our childhood behind and flung open the door to adulthood. Ready or not, there we were—officially on our own. We now held our future in our hands as we stepped out into the world to make our mark.

As we brought our own children to this threshold of adulthood, we assumed they would follow a path of independence and self-sufficiency similar to ours. We started taking steps to prepare ourselves—and them—for the time when we would let go and watch them fly off on their own.

To soften our grief, we began to dream and plan for life after the children were out of the nest. Travel. New careers. Fewer financial

obligations. Remodeling. Free time to enjoy our hobbies and interests. There would be tears of sadness from one eye and tears of
joy from the other as we set aside the role we had carried: parents
raising children.

Then the long-awaited, much anticipated day came and we realized the expectation of closing the chapter on parenthood was only
a myth. The reality? Parenting doesn't stop when our children grow
up. And the nest doesn't always empty when or how we thought it
would. Our children may or may not be sleeping under our roof. But
regardless, our sense of responsibility continues as we search for
understanding about this new identity: parents of adult children.

Now That They're Grown

A large percentage of our adult children ages eighteen to early
thirties and even beyond—sometimes referred to as Generation-
Xers, adultolescents, twenty-somethings, and emerging adults—are
successfully stepping out into their new roles as adults. They have
taken the necessary steps to prepare and are now creating a new
life for themselves both personally and professionally. They are
buying homes, managing their own finances, traveling, building
new relationships, perhaps starting families of their own. They
speak to us about their goals and passions along with their commitment and determination to seize all life has to offer. As parents,
we stand on the sidelines and cheer as we wonder how we fit into
this new picture, praying God will guide their steps along His plan
for their lives.

Some of our adult children, however, are not in as much hurry
to leave home. Others go but come back after graduation from
college or a failed relationship. There are those who can't find
a job, perhaps due to increasing competition in the marketplace.
Some find a job, but not the ideal job of their dreams or one that
will adequately cover their expenses. Many seem to be slower in

growing up and reaching a level of maturity to take charge of their future with confidence and responsibility.

Our children say they do care about their futures, but some wrestle to know how to make the dream of success become reality. As a result, many of them struggle with significant anxiety, pressure, and uncertainty. Even if they don't automatically turn to us for support, we want to do what we can to help.

Our Changing Role

No matter where they are on this journey into adulthood, we may find our adult children looking to us for insight, counsel, mentoring, and encouragement. They want to relate to us—adult to adult. We need to be ready and willing to make that shift with them. Whether or not we agree with the life choices they make, our responses to those choices can significantly affect their lives and our relationships with them. That's where our insecurities as parents may come to the surface.

> One size *doesn't* fit all when it comes to parenting our adult children.

Jane, a mom of a young adult, described it so clearly: "I'm struggling to find my place in my child's life right now. I find myself guessing a lot about the right way to help. I don't know how to step back yet stay connected. It's an awkward time for both of us."

Another bewildered mom captured the frustration we often feel as parents: "I know there's a time to speak and a time to keep silent. I just don't know which to do when!"

Today's parents may have dreams of their own for launching their children out of the nest and into adulthood, but we now recognize that one size *doesn't* fit all when it comes to parenting our adult children. We need to respond to each one individually as we evaluate their readiness to move into this new phase of life. Indeed, it's not just about the number of candles on the cake. We should consider their needs—emotional, physical, financial, educational, spiritual, and social—as we determine how to support them and cultivate a new relationship: adult to adult.

It's also important to evaluate our own definition of successful parenting. Author Stephen Bly contends that our success as parents "is not determined by [our children's] economic good fortune, scholastic achievements, social popularity, or how rapidly or slowly children pull away from their parents. . . . Successful parenting means you have helped your children become the persons God wants them to be."[1]

> Our challenge? To determine how we will channel our concern in ways that will support and encourage them to develop both self-sufficiency and a positive connection with family.

The question is not *if* we will be concerned. We love our children and will always be vested in their well-being. They may not be physically living at home, but we do see them as still in our emotional "family nest." Our challenge? To determine how we will channel our concern in ways that will support and encourage them to develop both self-sufficiency and a positive connection with family.

Our first step is to set aside our preconceived ideas and seek God's wisdom to understand our own children individually. We should ask questions and listen when they speak. They want to know we are behind them as they move into the role of adulthood. Our support coupled with their movement. We need to talk *with* them (not *at* them) as they develop their life plans and share from the wisdom of our experience. But it's important to acknowledge that it is their unique future they are creating, not our history for them to copy automatically.

We need to pray for them and with them. There may be fences to mend. We need to set boundaries while maintaining a connection as family. Our children long to know we love them—unconditionally. We need to be their strongest cheerleaders, celebrating their victories and supporting them through the struggles of life. We need to communicate openly, honestly, and respectfully, even when we disagree with their choices.

Just as we encourage them to take care of themselves to the best of their ability—physically, emotionally, and spiritually—we must do the same for our marriages and ourselves. We also face significant life changes, many similar to those of our adult children. We are closing the chapter on childhood activities we shared with them and now developing new interests, even new relationships. Many of us are contemplating career changes. Finances are taking a priority focus as we consider our current needs and look ahead to retirement. Some parents are dealing with relocation issues as they make plans to downsize into a new living space. Whatever your plans may be, know that changes are on their way.

About This Book

As parents of adult children, we are facing a variety of challenges as we negotiate our way through this passage of our lives. In the chapters ahead, we'll hear insight, encouragement, and strategies—*secrets*—for responding, from both parents and young adults. Several of them have shared from their personal experiences, and out of respect to their families, we have changed names and some details to protect their privacy. Marriage and family experts will also step in to offer wise counsel. At the close of each chapter, we will pause for you to reflect on your own personal story and consider how you will respond to the opportunities and challenges before you. You may want to join other parents to read and discuss the book together.

As the mother of two adult sons, my parenting world was male-oriented. That is, until one of my sons married a wonderful young woman. I've talked with many mothers who have raised daughters and we've discovered we share many joys and challenges in common. I refer to "he" throughout the book rather than "he/she" for brevity. Let your mind translate to your own parenting language as you consider the stories shared and apply the truths to your own life experiences.

For us, and our children, it is the dawn of a new day, time to begin another chapter in the relationship we are continually building with them. What will be reflected on the pages of our family's history? The days ahead will write the answer. The health and well-being of a relationship is dependent on each person's dedication and contribution to it. We cannot control how our children will respond to this changing relationship now that they have stepped into an adult role. They are responsible for their own choices.

The opportunity is ours to seek God's guidance in order to contribute our best offering as parents to our children. It is our calling and it is our blessing.

However, we do know this truth: The opportunity is ours to seek God's guidance in order to contribute our best offering as parents to our children. It is our calling and it is our blessing. And it will be an integral part of the legacy we leave for generations to come.

Join me in the pages ahead as we consider together how to contribute our very best as parents toward building a healthy relationship with our adult children . . . now that they're grown.

Chapter One

Step One: Know What You're Getting Into

*"To bring up a child in the way he should go,
travel that way yourself once in a while."*
—Josh Billings, humorist

Now that my son has finished his training, he is focused on building his own life and establishing himself. He wants to be totally independent and determined to make his own choices. I'm not quite sure how to relate to him now. How do I give the support I think he still needs while respecting his freedom and not meddling?

My daughter just graduated from college and wants to move back home. I thought she'd be getting a job and going on with her life, but she says she's not ready. I think she's afraid she can't make it, but that just doesn't seem like her. She's smart and has a lot of friends. You'd think she would want to get out and on her own. I don't understand.

My son is struggling with some choices I don't approve of. We've not always had the best relationship, and I don't want to push him away, but whenever I bring it up, he gets mad. When is he going to grow up and learn to do the right thing?

We've raised three children. The older two are on their own and doing great; but the youngest is in his mid-twenties and still at home. He has no ambition and says he doesn't know what he wants to do with his life. I think he's lazy. He should have a plan and be out on his own by now. His older brothers were by his age. I just don't get it.

I'm worried. My daughter seems to be very depressed but won't get help. She's in her late twenties, and this should be the most exciting time of life for her. I don't know what's wrong. What can I do?

As a counselor and life coach, I often hear cries for help like these from parents of adult children. Many are perplexed, unsure of what they are experiencing themselves, and feel clueless about their children's desires and needs. They describe a breakdown somewhere in their relationship with their children, and they are searching for tools to fix what seems to have fallen apart. Some come with a sense of anxiety, fearful of what may happen in the days ahead and feeling unprepared to respond. The problems may differ in scope, but there are some common denominators—concern about the child's situation coupled with a sense of urgency to restore, repair, or protect the relationship.

What do we do when we want to solve a problem or prevent one from occurring? When our car is not running properly, we don't simply pick up tools and start adjusting parts randomly. We must first understand how the car operates and what is needed for it to run properly. Then we can identify what the problem is and how to address it.

Our relationships with our adult children are no different. We must begin by understanding what life is like for them so we'll know what to expect and how to respond as challenges arise. Equipped with insight and empathy woven together with wisdom from the Lord, we'll know how to parent our adult children effectively.

Identifying Their Challenges

Young adults are dealing with the major developmental task of establishing their identity in today's society. They are looking in the mirror and realizing, "I'm not a kid anymore. So who am I now as an adult? And what is that supposed to look like?"

These young adults are ready to let go of the expectations, pressures, and limitations of adolescence to enjoy the freedom of independence as an adult. They see before them a blank canvas and a palette filled with a vast array of colors. The paintbrush is in their hands, and they can now begin to create the picture their minds have dreamed of and their hearts have longed for during those turbulent teen years. While they may have an idea of the type of masterpiece they want to create, they may not know how or where to begin. They do know, however, that they want it to be their own work of art and not simply a re-creation of their parents' life pictures.

> It is important to them to create their own identity.

It's not that they necessarily dislike or want to abandon their parents completely. It is important to them, however, to create their own identity. They want to establish their own value system and perspectives on life—apart from those of their parents. While at times this may seem to parents as if their adult children are disregarding their views and dismissing their advice, in fact, this declaration of independence is an important developmental stage. Our children now must learn how to make their own decisions, solve their own problems, and deal with the consequences of their choices.

Psychologists Lois and Joel Davitz identify this as a tense time as these young adults sort out many things about themselves:

> There's tension, but that makes sense. Having just taken a giant step from the shelter of the teen years onto the ladder of adulthood, their footing is far from secure. In fact, it's downright shaky. In their favor, however, is the buoyancy of youth, the belief in being invulnerable, and the prospect of endless tomorrows.... For the teen turned twenty, it is a brave new world to be discovered and experienced to the fullest.[1]

We watch as many of these new adults set goals, follow through on preparation and training, then step out boldly into the marketplace. They are determined to establish a strong foundation as they begin to climb that ladder toward success. They are intent on creating a positive identity, both professionally and personally.

While some adult children long for the day when they can be totally independent, they choose to remain at home and continue receiving their parents' assistance until they complete their plans and are ready to successfully move out on their own. They have a focus, goals, and intentions; and they look to their parents to help get them solidly on their feet. However, others have difficulty finding the confidence to step out on their own. They may lack a sense of direction of where or how to move forward with life. Or they may struggle with life challenges and question their ability to make it on their own. Emotional maturity develops at differing paces and through differing life experiences for our children as they transition from childhood to adulthood. Whatever their challenges may be, home offers safety and security.

Statistics on today's young adults indicate many struggle to cope with the challenges of adulthood. Psychologist Dr. Jane Adams identifies indicators of the problems our adult children have in adjusting:

- Twenty-eight percent of 21-year-olds have downsized the ambitions they had for themselves at [age] 18, and 50 percent of persons [ages] 21 to 30 believe their goals will never be accomplished.

- Fifty-eight percent of 21- to 24-year-olds live at home or have boomeranged back in the last two years; for 25- to 34-year-olds, the figure is 34 percent.

- Independent adulthood is achieved five to seven years later by young adults than it was in 1960.

- Forty percent of young adults [ages] 18 to 35 are excessively dependent on their parents for financial, emotional, and physical support.

- Over half the parents of 21- to 32-year-olds contribute a quarter or more to the income of their grown children, in money, goods, and services.[2]

We read statistics such as these, make a comment or two, and then go on about our day—unless those statistics are found within our own family relationships. Then we come face-to-face with reality. It is more than just facts and figures. In my counseling office, in my ties with friends and family, and in my own life as a parent, I see the reality of these statistics as young adult children and their parents work to push past the anxiety, confusion, frustrations, and broken hearts.

Young Adults Speak Out

If we really want to understand our adult children, we must listen to them with our minds and our hearts as they share their dreams and goals as well as their disappointments and concerns. They communicate much, through both their words and their silence.

When asked to describe the challenges they face, young adults identify a primary need to decide what they want in life and to figure out how to successfully turn that desire into reality. They are moving from the comfort of home and the routine of the classroom to the responsibilities of independence and the demands of the workplace. They describe the pressures of feeling responsible for themselves as they must establish their own structure and routine—finding and keeping a job, paying bills, cooking, covering medical needs, repaying school loans, and finding their own solutions to problems. Then there are those who also have responsibilities to a spouse and children.

> If we really want to understand our adult children, we must listen to them with our minds and our hearts as they share their dreams and goals as well as their disappointments and concerns.

I posed this question to a number of young adults: "What challenges are you facing as an adult right now?" Take a look into the window of their lives and hear some of the concerns they expressed:

Trying to get out on my own and being able to support myself rather than relying on my parents.

The stress of going to school full time and working full time to cover my expenses are my biggest worries right now.

My challenges? Finances, school concerns, marriage problems, friendship issues, job concerns, career choice, transportation problems, no support from my parents, who are divorced and fighting with each other. . . . The list goes on.

Trying to balance school, work, and my social life is hard for me.

I don't know what I want to do with my life.

There are so many decisions I have to make and so many choices. I wish someone would just tell me what to do. I used to say I wanted to make up my own mind but I need some help figuring it all out.

I live on my own with a roommate, but my parents still try to meddle in my life a lot. They call too much, drop by unannounced, and ask too many questions. They are always telling me what to do and don't listen to me. Then they get mad if I don't follow their advice. I love them but it's hard to handle that.

Living at home is hard for me. My parents still treat me as they did when I was in high school and don't see me as an adult. We fight a lot.

My parents give me money if I need something, but they don't have much time for me. I wish they would call sometimes, at least once a week. I'm sure they care, in their own way. I could just use the support right now. I really feel alone.

I know I'm twenty-four years old and should be out on my own, but I'm not sure I can make it without my parents around. I think life is hard.

I have a lot of decisions to make and don't feel I can go to my parents for advice. They told me once I got out of college I would have to make it on my own. I don't want them to think I'm a failure.

I thought when I graduated from college, I would land a great job making good money, but that's a lot harder than I expected. I'm living back at home and working at my dad's store until I find the right job.

I think I know what I want to do with my life, but my parents don't agree. I feel pressured that if I don't follow their plan, they won't support me. I feel stuck.

I've always heard this was supposed to be the best time of my life, and I couldn't wait. Now that I'm in my mid-twenties, I think life is harder. I'm about to graduate and be on my own. My parents tell me it's all up to me now, but I'm afraid of making wrong choices that will ruin my life. I'm not sure I'm ready.

My biggest challenges right now are getting back to church, furthering my career, and doing the right things.

Being a single adult woman is hard in today's times, making it on my own, getting my career going, and keeping myself safe.

Our Search for Understanding

As parents, we think we know our children well. After all, we gave birth to them and have been with them throughout their lives. We've seen them at their best, and we've witnessed them at their worst. We assume we know what makes them happy and what frustrates them. We think we know just what they are encountering at this stage of their lives. We reflect back on our own experiences, remembering how we stepped into our role as an adult, and we expect the same or more from our children. "When I was their age . . ." our thoughts begin, ending with, "So why can't they . . . ?"

There are, indeed, some similar challenges between our entry into adulthood and that of our children. Yet we may not always see the challenges and opportunities unique to today's young adults or remember some of the struggles we experienced as we took those first adult steps. As a result, many parents are frustrated with the actions or inactions of their adult children. They become irritated when their children won't consider their advice, follow their direction, or act in the manner they expect. They may see their children as selfish, immature, lazy, or rebellious, and they lash out in despair, "Now that you are an adult, act like one!"

Parents are looking for responsibility, independence, focus, and direction—indicators of adult maturity. However, their expectations may or may not be reasonable for their individual child. And their child may or may not share those same goals and expectations.

Moms Share Their Concerns

As we have identified, many of today's young adults are struggling with this new identity, which makes parents like Annette very anxious. "I see my daughter as wanting too much, too fast. She's a hard worker and will always justify that she can just 'work harder' to have the house, the cars, and the furniture. But I can see that she's growing weary—working a lot of overtime to pay for all of the 'things' she's acquired. She wants to have a baby in the next year or so, but finances might be an issue. I do notice that (as she grows more interested in having children) she's becoming closer to me, talking about 'girl things' more, etc. I enjoy these times with her. I imagine that when the babies start coming, we'll really come to understand what the word *challenges* means!"

Another mom has noticed the changes in her youngest daughter now that the older children have moved away. "I think she feels the burden of taking care of me, since I am adjusting to my older daughters being out of the house and establishing themselves as married young women. She checks on me a lot. I think she also may feel pressure to get engaged, since she is the last one of the girls."

"Finances are a big struggle for my son," notes the mom of a young man in his mid-twenties. "He wants to get married, but I don't know how he'll support a wife when he can barely make it himself."

27

In reflecting on her son's recent graduation from college, one mom made this observation: "When James was a little boy, he was so easygoing and laid back . . . not a stubborn bone in his body. He just wanted to enjoy life. Now that he is an adult, he may be too easygoing. While he's still intent on enjoying life, he doesn't seem to be in a hurry to get out on his own and on with his life. I wish he had a stronger sense of drive."

Carol, the mother of three adult sons in the military, sees the unique challenges many young adults are facing in transitioning from life in the military to civilian status. "One of my boys will discharge from the military this year and will face some significant adjustments to civilian life. He may need to move back home for a while, and that will involve adjustments for all of us."

Sometimes parents like Kim have broken hearts as they see their adult children in troubling life circumstances. "My daughter is married to a man who drinks too much and is very argumentative. She seems to be withdrawing into herself. I'm worried for her and for her baby."

Health problems, including mental health challenges such as depression, obsessive-compulsive disorder, anxiety, bipolar disorder, and eating disorders, sometimes surface in young adults as they face increasing life pressures. One mom describes the turmoil she witnesses in the life of her daughter trying to establish her independence while struggling with significant problems. "Our daughter has been diagnosed with bipolar disorder and has not been able to keep a steady job. She lived with us for a while after a divorce until she felt like she was ready to move back out on her own. She got herself set up with a new job and an apartment, determined to make it on her own. However, she has lost that job and is once again struggling financially. We just don't know what will happen next and how we should respond. It is a troubling pattern for all of us."

I recently sat with the mother of a twenty-year-old cancer survivor as her son prepared for surgery. With a heavy heart, she shared her burden for her son and the sadness she felt as she watched him deal with the challenges of this disease and its limitations on a significant time in his life. The protective side of her longs to step in and take charge of his care and his choices, while the understanding side of her realizes that as an adult, he can now make these important decisions on his own as he deals with life one day at a time. Heavy responsibilities for a young man just learning to embrace the role of an adult.

The Challenge for Parents

While the stories from these parents do identify some troubling challenges for our children, others relate the excitement and anticipation they feel as they watch their children begin a new chapter in life. Yet with that expectancy also come the uncertainties of how the future will unfold and what role parents are to play in the lives of their adult children. This is most evident when young adults don't move in the direction or at the speed parents deem appropriate in assuming their role and responsibilities as adults.

Whether or not they realize it, a sense of urgency may cause parents to push their adult children toward some type of action, even if it is not the best one for the child.

Then there are parents who approach their adult children with the perspective that "If I could make it on my own successfully, so can you." When their children reach a certain age or life event (typically eighteen, or just after graduation from high school or college), they step back from the support role. They do so whether or not their children are prepared and ready to assume all the responsibilities that come with being an independent adult. They take the "sink or swim" approach as their children jump off into the waters of adulthood, assuming they will learn best by figuring things out through trial and error as they go along. As a result, their children must take full care of themselves, ready or not.

Then there's another group of parents who view this turning point in their child's life in comparison to their own, but take a much different approach. They remember the struggles and challenges they encountered as they stepped into the role of adulthood and don't want their children to struggle. They want to give them more than what they had, so they take an active role in their children's lives, sometimes to the point of not letting go.

From their mouths, you'll hear phrases like, "Whatever you need, just ask and I'll make sure you have it." Or, "Take all the time you need to decide what you want to do. We'll take care of everything for you." There are those who believe they know what is best for their children's future and take a directive role in their children's choices. "We want you to be successful, so you need to listen to us and take our advice."

While there may be those days and circumstances that prompt us to want to walk away from our role, we know that we became parents the first time we took our children into our arms and we will remain in that role throughout our lives. Beyond the hurts, the confusion, and the uncertainties, there is a desire in the quiet places of our hearts to lovingly support our children. Our challenge is to discern how to offer support that is healthy both for our children and for ourselves.

Practical Tips for Parents

Understanding our adult children is the first step, *a critical step*, along this journey of parenting. It begins by viewing them— each one independently—as the unique individuals God created. He instilled in each one the capacity to love and be loved. He gave each one talent and abilities, strengths and limitations, and He has a plan for each of their lives. We need to set aside our own plans and dreams for our children's lives so we can be open to learn about theirs. We need to watch, listen, and ask questions as we learn about life from their perspectives. And we need to pray for them, asking God to show our children the plans He has for them. Perhaps that's one of the most difficult and yet most freeing tasks we have as parents—to let go of our sense of control and trust God to guide. As we do so, our children can then sense both the freedom and responsibility to take charge of their lives, knowing God is there to guide and we are alongside them with our love and support.

As we talk with them about their dreams and goals, we must be mindful that they are in a time of exploration and they don't necessarily have their futures all mapped out as we would hope. We need to respect the stress they are working through as they consider possibilities before them, and we must remember that the challenges they face today are not necessarily the same as those we encountered at their age. We must fight the urge to say, "I know just how you feel, so this is what you need to do."

It's also important to avoid minimizing their struggles or over-reacting to their stresses. We need to acknowledge their concerns without a barrage of commentary and offer our confidence in their ability to successfully work through their challenges.

As we talk with them, we must be careful to withhold comments that may appear judgmental and avoid comparisons with other children—their siblings, their friends, our friends' children. Again, keep in mind that each person is unique and must find their own individual measure of success as they choose the path they will follow.

Remember, the goal in this type of conversation is to gather information so we can better understand our children before deciding how to respond in a way that respects the relationship. That means we must *listen*—with our mind and our heart—as they share their perspectives, their needs, their concerns, their hopes, and their dreams. In the following chapter, we'll talk more about how to communicate effectively and support our children as they work through the challenges, choices, and changes they are encountering.

> It's important that we foster a spirit of hopefulness in ourselves and in them.

Our responsibility—to God and to our children—is to meet them where they are and to recognize the talents and abilities He has instilled in them, as well as the challenges they are facing. It's important that we foster a spirit of hopefulness in ourselves and in them. Then we can learn how to express our love and offer our insight and encouragement in meaningful, supportive ways as they travel this journey into adulthood.

On a Personal Note

Reflect back to your own life experiences as a young adult.

How was life in our society different/similar to today?

What challenges did you face?

What opportunities were available to you?

What helpful support did you receive from your parents or other adults?

Think about each of your adult children—individually.

What do you observe in their lives right now—both opportunities and challenges?

What are they communicating/not communicating to you?

Find a time to talk with your adult children, one to one. Express both your intent to understand their desires and their needs and your commitment to learn how to support them effectively as you learn how to parent an adult. Then listen. Just listen.

Pray for God's wisdom as you seek to understand life for your adult children and for His guidance and protection of them as they begin this new chapter in their lives.

Chapter Two

Be Their Coach Without
Taking Charge

*"Listen to the desires of your children. Encourage them and
then give them the autonomy to make their own decision."*
—DENIS WAITLEY, AUTHOR AND MOTIVATIONAL SPEAKER

We stood there together, looking around at the apartment that would
be my son's new home. "I think this will work out fine for you," I
said confidently. "We can put your table and chairs in that corner
and your television across the room. Then we can place your desk
right here and set the other things around. I have a couple of lamps
that will be perfect in here. Then in the kitchen, I think we'll take
those curtains down and get something more suited for you. It won't
take us long at all to have this place looking great."

I fluttered around the apartment, planning the details of how we
would set things up for his first place on his own, when I glanced
over and saw the look on his face. If you are a parent of an adult
child, you know the look. It's the I-don't-mean-any-disrespect-but-
I-have-my-own-ideas look that told me I had stepped over the line.
After all, it was *his* new place and *he* was in charge, not me.

But I'm the one with the decorating sense, I thought as I quickly came to my own defense. *I know what will work best and I can save him time and energy if he'll just take my advice.*

Once again, I needed to remember that while I may have ideas about how things should be for my children, they have their own ideas as well. I needed to take off my Mother-knows-best hat and put on my coach's hat so I could offer suggestions while acknowledging that he was ultimately in charge. I needed to be able to share my advice in a way that wasn't threatening or pressuring while respecting his right to make his own choices, which may not always be like mine. I also needed to remember that there's a time to speak and a time to keep silent. I was faced with the question of what was more important: my opinion or the opportunity for him to take ownership of his new home.

That afternoon the challenge was about decorating an apartment, so it was a bit easier to let go. Other times, however, when the life choices are more significant, it's harder to stay on the sidelines and watch, knowing some decisions will bring success and others may create problems. The protective parent in me wants to jump in and take charge, yet I know in my heart that's not best for them in the long term. I have to learn to wait for open doors to share my thoughts and then express them in a way that is suggestive rather than directive.

Two things help me keep the proper perspective in times like that. First, I remember that I learned a lot by trial and error, and my children will as well. Second, and most important, I have assurance that while I may be on the sidelines of their lives, God is right in the midst of the game with them. He will guide, direct, and protect them as long as they ask Him to do so. Once we are clear in our roles, we can then focus on how to communicate with our children as they learn to take charge of their own lives, respecting their needs as well as ours. With God's guidance, we can communicate our concerns and the wisdom of our experience while also respecting our children's desire to design their own lives.

Coaching offers an approach that can help facilitate productive conversation and strengthen relationships. When you coach someone, you help the person expand his vision, build confidence, and increase skills as he takes steps toward reaching his goals. You offer yourself as a confidant, encourager, accountability partner, and mentor. In a positive coaching relationship there is shared respect, honesty, and trust as you work toward a mutual goal.

> In a positive coaching relationship there is shared respect, honesty, and trust as you work toward a mutual goal.

Traditional coaches in areas like sports, the arts, and competitive endeavors set goals and direct the process as they work with their athletes and performers. They are in charge. Life coaches differ in that they take on the role of facilitator, helping others reach their goals in the best possible way. The people they coach cast their vision and identify their own goals. The coaches are there to support them and help them keep their intentions in focus as they move from desires and dreams to success and fulfillment. These coaches are ready with encouragement, information, honest feedback, and resources as their clients seek their assistance.

Many of the young adults I work with in my counseling practice seek help in how to embrace this new role of adult as they begin to take charge of their own lives. They want to learn how to establish independence while maintaining a relationship with their parents. They don't want to appear disrespectful if they go against their parents' advice, and they want the freedom to make the choices they believe are right for them. It is a challenging task for them as well as for the parents, who must learn to let go of the reins and adapt to this new season of life.

When you ask them what they are looking for, most young adults respond with a similar list: respect, acceptance, someone to listen (with a goal of understanding), advice when asked, independence that allows them to make choices and deal with consequences, encouragement, and the freedom to cast their own vision for their future. Along with that list, I would add the value of parents showing patience and restraint, giving grace, and bathing all these things with unconditional love. Our children need to know we love them for who they are, not for what they do or don't do. Sometimes we are pleased with their behavior and other times concerned. Yet our love flows consistently, without condition. These gifts we can offer our children are important tools to help them successfully move through this time of transition into adulthood.

Their Vision, Not Ours

We have dreams and aspirations for our children; we believe we know how their future should unfold and what they need to accomplish *our* goals for them. We think we know what is best, and in our eagerness to see the results we hope for, we may tend to push, direct, and pressure. Oh, we don't mean to. But after all, we have the experience, and we want them to have the best future we can imagine for them. All too often, however, our children don't share the same vision. They have their own ideas about how they want their future to unfold.

As a young adult woman preparing for college, I had two high school teachers who firmly believed I should major in engineering. They were convinced I would do quite well, and my parents jumped on that bandwagon with them, confident I would find success. While I appreciated their belief in me, I didn't share their vision. But I didn't want to disappoint. So off I went to begin my studies. In between the science and mathematics courses, I managed to squeeze in a couple of electives and found them to be such a breath of fresh air, I couldn't wait for those classes, and as you might expect, they drew my strongest grades.

One afternoon I sat with the professor of one of those classes to talk about my career goals. I shared about the path that I was encouraged to follow. He listened to what I said—and what I didn't say—and then began to ask some powerful questions. If I could look ahead five or ten years and felt the freedom to design my own future, what would I want in that picture? It didn't take long to admit that it was not a career in engineering. It felt almost disrespectful in one regard to say that, and oh so freeing in another. Could I chart my own course and not lose the relationships that were important to me? Would they understand? Would they support me?

He continued to ask questions about what I wanted in life and allowed me freedom to cast my own vision and set goals on how to accomplish the passion of my heart. He listened with a desire to understand, gave his opinion when I asked, and offered suggestions to think about. He drew from his own life experiences and offered insight as he encouraged me to grant myself freedom to search my heart and seek God's direction. He gave some cautions to consider, which I took as suggestions rather than directives because he had set a stage of support and respect. His coaching that afternoon changed the course of my life.

That's what our adult children are looking for in us—a coach to mentor and encourage them as they cast their vision for their lives and then determine how to chart their course and find their own unique measure of success. They need our honesty and can benefit from our insight and experiences if we can communicate those things in a non-threatening manner. Shifting the role from director to coach will encourage a healthy adult-to-adult relationship as we all transition to this new phase of our lives.

The Gift of Listening

If you are one of those people who sits through commercials on television without channel surfing, you probably recognize the scene: A young man wandering around, cell phone in hand, verifying the efficiency of the system he's depending on to carry his message to the listener: "Can you hear me now?" Funny how simple phrases like that can stick in our minds and then roll off our lips—exactly what the advertising company is hoping will happen.

Behind all the humor, however, is a significant question that bears our consideration, because listening is one of the most important gifts we can give our adult children as we forge this new relationship with them. It is a powerful attribute to an effective coaching relationship.

Have you ever tried to talk with someone—hoping they would listen, support, and understand—only to walk away feeling confused, angry, disappointed, and disillusioned? More than likely, you didn't make the connection you wanted to. You didn't think you were heard. You walked away wondering, *What was the point?*

> Our children don't want us to talk *at* them: They want us to talk *with* them.

Of course, when we picture ourselves as a speaker not being heard, we can relate wholeheartedly to the frustrations. But what about when the tables are turned? How often do we, as listeners, send others away with those very same feelings? Our intentions are well meaning. Yet we sometimes miss the mark as an active, effective listener.

As I counsel young adults, I hear this complaint often: "My parents don't listen to me." Unfortunately, that is too often the case. We may hear their words, at least enough to catch the gist of what they are saying, but what they want most is for us to listen—with our hearts. To hear the words and hear what they are saying with their posture, their facial expression, and their tone of voice. Do we listen to hear what we want to hear? Or do we listen with a true intent to understand? Our children don't want us to talk *at* them: They want us to talk *with* them. To do so, we must listen with our hearts.

Listening is perhaps one of the best gifts we can give our children. While some people tend to be masterful listeners intuitively, listening is a skill that can be developed with attention and practice. A new mother tunes in to even the faintest sounds from her infant. A musician trains his ear to improve his performance. Schoolchildren learn to listen carefully to their teacher's instruction. We have that ability, and yet so many times we don't really listen. Why?

A number of things may slip into our mental mindset and distract us. As I mention a few, take a moment to consider your own blocks to active listening:

- Assumptions—thinking we know what our child is going to say. This can lead to mentally "tuning out" before he is finished talking, or interrupting and finishing his sentence as we interpreted it.

- Twisting a message to make it say what we want. We hear what we want to hear, not necessarily what is being said; and we tune out what we don't want to hear. We may miss the point entirely.

- Our own emotions can become a distraction or lead to wrong conclusions. Along this same line, if we have an offensive or defensive attitude, we can't honestly listen and consider what is being communicated. Our mind is planning our response and our mouth is just waiting for an opportunity to begin moving.

- Ignoring nonverbal cues can lead us to wrong conclusions about what we hear, and our own cues may send a message to the speaker that we're not tuned in. Notice that a large percentage of our communication is nonverbal—eye contact, facial expression, gestures, posture, and tone of voice. The smallest impact is often in the actual words we speak.

- Distractions—both external and internal—can create problems. The noise around us and the thoughts racing through our minds can draw our focus away. Our children live busy lives. So do we. It's vital that when we take time for conversation with them, they know they have our undivided attention. This may mean scheduling uninterrupted time to talk. When we do so, we communicate their importance and our desire to connect with them.

- We may have our own agenda for the conversation, so we find ourselves interested and available only for what fits that focus. We want to be sure our children hear what we have to say, but we're not really interested in their thoughts. We just do what we need to do and say what we need to say to get the job done and move on to the next thing on the list.

Yet when we do listen—*really listen*—we give a gift to our children who have trusted us enough to share their thoughts: Respect. Desire to understand. Willingness to consider what has been shared. Interestingly enough, when we give these gifts, often we receive them in return. Everyone wins.

Time and attention are two precious gifts you have to offer others when you listen. The results reach far beyond the topic of the moment. It takes desire. It takes focus. It takes practice. Begin by listening to the music on your radio. Listen to your child. Listen to your spouse. Listen to your fellow employees at work. Listen to the clerk at the checkout counter. Listen to your neighbor. Listen to the birds. Listen to your own heart. Listen to God. Take time out to set aside the busyness of life and just listen—with your mind, your body, and your heart. Then when your child says, "Can I talk to you?" you'll smile and say with confidence, "I'm listening!"

Powerful Questions

One of the successful aspects of the life coaching relationship is found in the coach's ability to ask powerful questions that challenge the client to find clarity and determine action steps. Rather than give the information and direct the thought process, coaches ask open-ended questions that create the possibility for new perspective in such a way that clients own their discovery. They are more empowered to take action if they have worked the process through in their minds and have developed their own action plan. They are also more likely to celebrate their successes and learn from their failures. The coach's role is to help facilitate that process and support them in a way that helps them achieve their goal and move forward toward the vision they have for their lives.

> Coaches ask open-ended questions that create the possibility for new perspective in such a way that clients own their discovery.

Our adult children are looking to us for guidance and support along with the acknowledgment that they are now in charge of their decisions and the consequences of their choices. They are beginning to look ahead and develop their own vision for their lives, set goals, and take action steps to move them toward the success they desire. Our position has shifted from leading in front or pushing from behind to walking beside them on their journey. They can benefit from our insight and experience if we know how and when to offer those tools. They can also find valuable life lessons through their own personal trials and errors. Healthy adult relationships have both of those elements present.

When we offer respect, understanding, and restraint, they will be more apt to ask our advice. If we listen to them first, they will be more apt to listen to us. I've found the following questions to be helpful conversation prompts when coaching clients on various life management issues. They may help you coach your child toward greater insight and positive steps as you walk beside him, guiding while empowering. As you consider these suggestions, you'll want to choose a phrasing style that best suits you and your child:

If you want him to clarify something he is telling you: Begin by telling him you want to understand but are not quite sure what he is saying. That way, he knows the goal is to seek understanding, not to be argumentative. Then ask:

- What do you mean by that?

- Tell me more.

- Help me understand.

- Will you give me an example?

If you want to encourage him to explore options:

- Would you like to brainstorm this idea?

- What other options can you think of?

- What have you tried so far?

- Have you explored any other possibilities?

If he's evaluating an option and considering its possibilities:

- Do you think this is good or bad or in-between? In what ways?

- How does this fit with your other plans, your lifestyle, and your beliefs?

- How will you know when you've reached your goal? What will it look like?

- If you choose this option, what would it mean for you now and in the future?

- What do you need to know to help you decide?

- What resources are available to help you?

- In the larger scheme of things, how important is this to you?

- If you choose this option, what will you need in order to follow through? Are you prepared?

If he is anticipating something:

- What might happen?

- What do you think are the chances for success?

- What if it doesn't work out the way you anticipate?

- Have you considered a backup plan if it doesn't work?

If you are helping him look at how to achieve a goal:

- What kind of action plan do you need to create to accomplish this?

- What support will you need?

- What will you do to begin? When will you begin?

- What could get in your way, and how will you deal with that obstacle?

When he's evaluating an experience:

- What lessons will you take away from this?

- How would you summarize this experience for yourself?

- If the same choice came up again, what would you do?

If you want to talk with him about taking action:

- What's your plan? How do you see it unfolding?

- Is this the best time to take action?

- Where do you go from here?

- What are your next steps and what will you need?

If he's struggling with a problem or seems stuck:

- What seems to be the problem?

- What concerns you most?

- What's getting in your way or holding you back?

- What have you tried so far?

- What do you need to get unstuck and move forward?

If you want to give advice:

- I'd like to share some thoughts, if you're open to hearing them.

- Something to consider might be . . .

- Have you thought about . . . ?

- I wonder if it would be helpful to . . .

- I'd like to suggest you consider . . .

- Will you please think about . . . ?

When More Direction Is Necessary

As much as we want and need to grant our adult children freedom to make their own choices and work through their own challenges, there are times when we need to step in with a more direct approach. For example, when we are providing financial assistance in areas such as education, medical, and automobile expenses, or when they are still living in our home.

It's important to be careful that we don't come across as demanding or threatening. Instead we need to set clear guidelines about our expectations and our assistance as we communicate the message to our children, "My love for you is unconditional; it is not based on your behavior or your choices. However, my level of assistance depends in part on the responsibility you are willing to take on. So let's talk about how we can work together."

While we often talk in generalities about taking responsibility and helping out, it is important to be clear about our expectations. Rather than saying, "I need you to help around the house while you are living here," be more specific: "We are living here together, so each of us needs to take on some responsibilities. I want you to____, and I will____." Also be clear about time frames. For example, "I want you to cover your car expense, which is due on____." Or, "You will need to take care of____by____."

Clarify any expectations you have that will determine your assistance. For example, if you are uncertain about helping with college expenses when grades are a concern, you might say, "When I see your satisfactory grades from the past semester, then I'll provide the financial assistance for the next one." Or, if you want to be certain your child will contribute toward expenses, you might explain, "When you have saved your portion of the amount due, I will contribute the part I've agreed to."

Try to avoid the message, "I can't____because____." Instead, use the approach, "I *can* help you *when* I see you taking responsibility for your life and when I am comfortable supporting your choices." The first statement is negative and implies a door has been closed, while the second assumes positive steps can be taken.

Our older son lived at home for a short time in between college and medical school, and our younger son lived at home after college for a while. In both cases, my husband and I needed to talk with our sons about our expectations and theirs. We were glad to help them out at those times in their lives. However, we also knew they needed to do all they could to manage things to the best of their abilities. When we were clear, things worked well. If we left expectations vague, we were more subject to misunderstandings. Healthy relationships have open, honest, respectful communication, particularly when it comes to expectations. And they establish boundaries, which we'll talk about in a later chapter.

As we look at coaching principles here, you might consider writing a contract to establish an agreement between you and your child. It can clarify expectations and set goals both of you will agree to follow, as one adult to another adult, and provide a reference point if there are misunderstandings later. For example, you might say, "I am glad to offer you some help, if we can agree to an arrangement that will work for us both. Let's make a contract that we both can abide by—something that identifies each of our responsibilities and expectations as well as consequences. We'll put it in writing so we'll both be clear and accountable to follow through."

Coach Germaine Porché of Eagle's View Consulting comments on the value of a coaching contract to help resolve relationship conflicts: "The coaching contract distinguishes the boundaries, outcomes, and timeline for the coaching relationship. People operate from written and verbal contracts—we recommend getting contracts in writing with signatures and all. It signifies commitment, and for some reason puts the heat on accountability and responsibility."

Agreements, whether written or verbal, may serve as a catalyst to help you establish an understanding with your adult child regarding financial responsibility and accountability, or perhaps home life concerns you need to address. Remember, an effective agreement—coach-to-client or parent-to-adult-child—focuses on a common goal of mutual understanding, respect, and cooperation: three important aspects of a healthy relationship.

There are times when our concerns seem to warrant some comments, yet we are not sure how to share our thoughts and give advice without appearing as if we are taking charge. Our fears seem to challenge our respect for their independence. Maryanne shared with me a recent experience where she found herself in this very situation:

> Our daughter-in-law recently had a serious health problem. Her parents and I were going crazy—trying to figure out how to give her much-needed advice, without intruding on her (and our son's) privacy and personal choices. It was very difficult, because there were long-term consequences to her health because of decisions the young couple made. Agonizing! At one point I did step in; I went down to spend a week with the young couple. I back-doored the kids—pulling the visiting nurse aside to say, "They're not stupid; they're ignorant of what they need to know and what they don't know. Please explain everything and point out things they may be missing."
>
> The nurse thanked me for telling her that fact and made it a point to be more thorough and involved in my daughter-in-law's care, which made a huge difference. I also explained to the kids that when I visit a doctor, I carry a list of questions to ask, so I can remember what I want to know. They thought that was a good idea, but had never considered doing it before. They simply didn't know and needed some pointers.
>
> *Pointers* are what they needed; they did not need to be told *what* to do—that was their choice. I took great care to phrase my statements in ways that did not lecture, but did provide information, and then left whatever they chose to do up to them.

Frequently, I say things like, "This is what I personally have observed in the past. It may pertain to you or it may not. You do whatever you feel you need to do, but this is something you might want to consider."

And then I let it be. I don't rehash choices they've made. I don't blame them if something they've done turns out poorly. I try to ask open-ended questions: "What do you think you might have done differently in this situation for a better outcome?" I want them to learn to evaluate their own lives and decisions—because I'm not going to be there for their whole lives.

Become the Coach Your Children Will Value

> They need to seek God's leadership and then look to us as their mentor, coach, and encourager.

In *Coaching by the Book*, L. Cecile Adams identifies the characteristics of an effective spiritual coach. These attributes are important to a coach/client relationship and can also be helpful tools as parents shift into a coaching role with their adult children. As you read this list, ask God to show you the traits He wants to cultivate in you to offer to your adult children. They will be some of the most precious gifts you can give them.

An effective coach affirms, asks questions, assists in planning, assists in skill development, celebrates, challenges, clarifies, encourages, guides, has integrity, hears with the heart, is caring, is confident, is faith-full, is grace-full, is objective, listens, provides connections, offers feedback, reconciles, seeks truth, shares wisdom, bears God's light.[1]

Our children are stepping into a future filled with challenges, opportunities, possibilities, success, failure, hopes, and fears. It's their time to take charge of their lives, cast their unique vision for the future, define their personal measure of success, and chart their own course. They don't need us to be in control. They need to seek God's leadership and then look to us as their mentor, coach, and encourager. As parents, we must ask God to help us embrace this new role, confident that as we seek Him, He will guide our children and guide us in the days ahead.

On a Personal Note

What challenges and opportunities is your adult child currently facing?

As you consider the characteristics of an effective coach, what areas would you like to focus on that would improve your effectiveness as a mentor, coach, and encourager to your child?

What action steps will you take to apply those characteristics in your relationship with your adult child?

Chapter Three

Create a Fresh Start

"Have a heart that never hardens, a temper that never fires,
and a touch that never hurts."
—CHARLES DICKENS

"Relationships are hard work."

I've made this statement countless times in my counseling office while working with clients struggling with relationships—most often within their families. I've made that same statement many times to the woman I see in the mirror. If we love each other enough, we should be able to get along and live happily ever after. Shouldn't we? Hmmm. That may be the case in fairy-tales we read as children, but real-life experiences tell us otherwise.

As much as we love our children and train them up in the way they should go, they aren't perfect. Consequently, they make many mistakes along the way. Sometimes it's spilling a drink on the kitchen floor just after we mopped it. Sometimes it's forgetting to tell us they left the gas gauge reading "empty" after they drove our car. Sometimes it's arguing with us and throwing a temper tantrum when we say no to their request. Sometimes it involves defiantly crossing boundaries by disrespecting our rules, our property, and even our reputation by rebelling against the very principles we stand for. Then there are times that are much more serious. Times that test our patience, tolerance, forgiveness, and unconditional love—beyond what we ever thought possible.

An honest look in the mirror tells us that as hard as we try to do the right things with our children, we aren't perfect either. At times we, too, miss the mark. No matter how many books we read or how much training we have, our life experience tells us that parenting is perhaps the most difficult job in the world, and we don't always make the best choices. There are some issues we foresee and prepare for, while other situations come along that catch us completely off guard. And we don't always cope as well as we'd like.

If we are in a difficult relationship with a co-worker and can't or don't want to deal with the problems involved, we can walk away and find another job. If we don't get along well with a friend, we may choose to no longer have any contact with that person and cultivate other friendships. If we don't like the service at a restaurant, we can choose to eat somewhere else. If we get frustrated, disappointed, or disillusioned with people, we can sometimes simply close the door of our homes and our hearts, disconnect, and walk away.

> We are responsible to do all we can to encourage positive, healthy relationships with our children.

None of this works with our children. We can choose not to listen to them. We can pull back emotionally. We can even put some distance between us. But we are their parents—for life. Regardless. The relationship we have with them may have its ups and downs, and we may not always experience the closeness we would like. But the ties that bind us are strong, and our role as parents doesn't stop because things aren't going well.

The truth is, as parents, we can't make our children like us. We can't make them agree with us. We can't make them spend time with us or take our advice. And we can't make them forgive us when we make mistakes. We can't control our children's choices or how they choose to view our relationship with them. So we're not entirely responsible for the relationship. We alone can't make it work.

We *are,* however, responsible to do all we can to encourage positive, healthy relationships with our children. That task was given to us the day we first held them in our arms, and it continues to be ours today. At times, that may mean taking the lead toward mending fences when problems come along that separate us. To be the ones to step up and close the door on the past and open the way for a new beginning toward a stronger family tie. Not always an easy task, but an important one. God holds us accountable to give our best offering to the relationships He has entrusted to us.

When Fences Break Down

Breakdowns occur in our relationships with our children when choices are made that disappoint and when misunderstandings or disagreements split us apart. In the midst of hurt, disappointment, and confusion, we struggle to find acceptance, tolerance, forgiveness, and respect—the tools that help us restore the connection in spite of our differences.

Suzanne came to my counseling office asking for help for her family. Her son had left home after a series of problems that had broken her heart. She and her husband had lost contact with him for several months and didn't know if they'd ever see him again. Then one evening, very unexpectedly, she received a call. One she had longed for but wasn't sure how to respond to.

> Billy was a good kid when he was young. He went to church, had good friends, did okay in school, never got into any real trouble. I don't know what happened after he went away to college, but he got involved in some things that really broke my heart. I couldn't believe it. His father and I talked to him and warned

55

him about the consequences but he wouldn't listen. The more we begged and pleaded, the more he resisted and turned his back on his family, his education, and a promising future—even on God. I was hurt and ashamed, and I felt like such a failure as a parent. I should have done more, or maybe less. I don't know. I was afraid for him as well. Unfortunately, he had to find out the hard way that with bad choices come difficult consequences.

Now he wants to come back home, get a job, finish his education, and start over. He says things are different and he's getting his life on track. I hope he's right but I wonder . . . I do want him to have that second chance at a good life and I want our family back together, but how do I let go of all that pain? Am I just supposed to forget the past? What he did? What he said to us when he stormed out of the house and out of our lives? Can I let my guard down and trust him again? Can I do a better job as a mother? I don't know how, but I'm going to have to figure out a way to deal with my feelings so we can move on. I believe God has forgiven him, but now I have to forgive him and forgive myself as well. I don't want to lose him again.

Suzanne must work through her hurts and fears, even misplaced feelings of failure, to find the forgiveness and willingness needed to rebuild her relationship with her son. Peggy has also experienced a sense of failure as a result of a strained relationship with her child. Like many well-meaning parents, she wanted a close relationship with her daughter, but her pressure for closeness resulted in more distance. Now she's struggling to mend the breakdown between them.

I used to think I was doing a good job as a mom. At least I was trying to be sure my daughter had what she needed and wanted growing up. I know I wasn't perfect, but I tried to do the right things with her. I went to all her games and performances. I got to know all her friends and got involved in everything she did. Maybe I tried too hard and pushed my relationship with her too far. In my effort to be part of whatever she was doing, I may have gone overboard. I think instead of encouraging her I smothered her and she began to pull back. She moved out on her own before she was really ready. Before I was ready.

I guess I was afraid if we didn't talk every day and do a lot together that I'd lose her. Now I hardly see or talk to her at all. I think my life revolved a lot, maybe too much, around her life. She knew that, even though I didn't. If only I would have backed off some and recognized what she needed. . . . If only I would have listened when she tried to tell me I was smothering her. . . . If only I would have done more for myself. . . . If only . . .

I now realize I made some mistakes and I want to change things between us. I know I can't go back and correct what I did, but I want her to know I will try to do a better job of respecting her need for independence. And I'll learn to do things for myself, too, without being afraid I'll lose her. To find some balance that will work for both of us. I just need to figure out how to tell her those things, ask her forgiveness, and get her to give our relationship another chance.

Whether the strain in the relationship came as a result of our choices as parents or those of our children, or perhaps a combination of both, we must do all we can to mend the fence—to let go of the past and move forward with a fresh start and a new commitment to contribute all we can toward forging a healthy relationship.

Letting Go

It sounds so simple, yet sometimes requires so much of us, especially when the weight of hurt and disappointment, of fear and anxiety, of pain and heartache crushes our spirits. How do you let go when someone hurts you deeply? How do you let go of feelings of failure and guilt? Some things can be easily set aside and forgotten so we can move on without any problem. Fresh starts come easily then.

But there are other rifts that occur in our relationships that seem to leave us shattered and wondering if we'll ever be able to let go and move on. And yet if we don't find a way to do so, we hold on to those feelings and they begin to take root and grow bitterness, resentment, discouragement, and shame. We hold on to memories that play over and over and over again in our minds, causing fresh wounds to our hearts with each replay and deeper separation with those we love.

If we have experienced hurts and disappointments from our children that we don't resolve, we may find it hard to draw close, to let our guard down and trust them. A wall goes up that separates us emotionally if not physically. Our children sense it and we do as well. Psychologist Dr. Jane Adams challenges us to consider our goal as we approach problems with our adult children.

> If our goal is to seek revenge on our kids or convince them to see things our way, or to hold on to conflict, pain, and anger until they see the error of their ways, we are likely to remain estranged from them. When our hopes are tempered with a more realistic assessment of what might still be possible in our relationships with them, if not in their lives, it is easier to let go of our fear, resentment, and anger while still continuing to love them—the very essence of forgiveness.[1]

If, on the other hand, we know we caused the break in the relationship, our guilt may bring on a sense of failure and a spirit of shame that makes us pull away. If these feelings go unresolved, they can breed a lack of confidence that may prompt us to become too permissive or too passive out of fear of repeating mistakes. This opens the door to actions we may later regret as we internalize emotions and adopt attitudes that can destroy us. We may freeze up in our fears or spend our time trying to make up for past errors. The end result is that our relationships with our children, our spouse, and even with God will suffer.

Letting go: It requires that we stop holding on to our thoughts and especially our emotions about what happened. To stop replaying the scenes and reopening the wounds. I remember watching a football playoff game with my husband, hoping the players on our favored team would do well and win. During the game one of the players made what later proved to be a costly mistake. The broadcaster replayed the scene over and over as the announcers discussed what went wrong. They even pointed out other mistakes in comparison. The more we watched the replay and heard the analysis, the more the picture burned in our memory, leaving us thinking of the mistakes more than the positive plays in the game. All the negativity led the announcers—and eventually their audience—to question the player's value on the team.

After the game ended, we watched as the media said to the player who made the error, "Tell us about what happened." He gave a brief, respectful answer before moving away from the camera, but I wonder if he would rather have replied, "I feel bad enough that we lost. Do we have to relive that one play? Can't we talk about what I did well in the game?" I imagine he was trying to figure out how to shake off what went wrong and move ahead rather then being reminded over and over about it. I suppose the protective part of me thought it was time to stop the replays—time to let it go.

> "What's more important? What went wrong and who was to blame, or how we can move beyond what happened toward a better, stronger, healthier relationship?"

Rewinding a tape and reviewing what happened may be helpful if we want to learn from our mistakes and develop a plan to avoid them in the future, but at some point replaying problems over and over in our minds or in conversation only burns those negative feelings deeper and deeper. It tethers us to the past and keeps us from confidently moving forward with a clear mind and heart. We have to ask ourselves, "What's more important? What went wrong and who was to blame, or how we can move beyond what happened toward a better, stronger, healthier relationship in the days ahead?"

Author Stephen Bly gives a great illustration of the importance of considering what we focus on when we find ourselves somewhere we don't want to be. It has been a good reference point for me several times as I have found myself in the midst of problems that needed resolving, particularly those that involve relationships.

> If you are driving to Phoenix and end up lost somewhere at the end of a gravel road north of Dusty, New Mexico, you can spend the next three days trying to figure out whether you made a wrong turn in Albuquerque, your spouse read the map wrong, the guy at the service station gave you the wrong advice, the government road signs were misleading, or it was just your destiny to spend the rest of your life in the Cibola National Forest.
>
> But the smart thing is to figure out how to get back to a highway and on your way to Phoenix. You will arrive much later than expected, and you might very well miss some events in the delay, but you will get there.[2]

Time for a Fresh Start

We have a loving heavenly Father who offers us forgiveness when we come to Him and ask. His heart is overflowing with mercy and grace for His children as He picks us up when we fall down and gives us a fresh start. He also commands us to forgive others. Forgiving someone or asking for forgiveness is not about emphasizing blame or justifying wrongs; it's not dependent on someone's remorse, and it doesn't require that we forget about what happened. It is about acknowledging what took place and granting freedom to let go and move ahead with the goal of offering a fresh start and hopefully building a stronger bond.

There's power in forgiveness. There's freedom in forgiveness.

There's love in forgiveness. It's a critical step in healing our relationships so we can move forward. And it begins in our minds and our hearts.

The first step toward a fresh start is to identify what caused the breach in the relationship and take an honest look at your feelings so you can open the door to forgiveness. Find safe, confidential ways to acknowledge what happened and work through the emotions you have about it. Journal. Talk to someone confidentially—a trusted friend, partner, pastor, or counselor—who can help you work through your emotions. Don't vent to your child or his spouse. Exercise. Rest. Cry if you need to. Laugh if it helps. Spend time talking to the Lord and reading His Word. Healing begins there. Hope begins there. The process of forgiving and letting go begins there.

Once you've begun to get a handle on your emotions, then you can discern what you need to do to move beyond the problem and on with life. Sometimes it involves simply setting aside the past and moving forward with a spirit of forgiveness and with renewed energy toward the relationship. It may involve a plan to approach some things differently. There are times when God does His work within us but does not direct us to talk about it with our children. Instead, He refines us in the fire and then allows our actions and the spirit we reflect to communicate our resolve to let go and our desire to move ahead toward a fresh start—a new beginning. Other times we need to talk with our child.

If You Have Been the One to Cause a Strain

If you know or suspect you have done or not done something that may have caused a strain in your relationship, it may be beneficial to talk to your child about what took place. Begin by asking God to work in your heart and your child's—to open a door of opportunity, to prepare you both for that conversation, and to set a tone for healing. Then choose a time and place that is private and will allow ample opportunity for you to talk without interruption. You may want to tell your child ahead of time that you'd like to talk about something and ask when it would be convenient. If he doesn't want to talk, then consider writing your thoughts in a letter or e-mail to him, so you can communicate your willingness to take responsibility and your desire to do what you can to make things right.

Begin by letting your child know that your desire is to have a positive relationship with him and that you know you have not always made the best choices as a parent. Let him know you don't want him to hold on to any unresolved hurts that would impact his life and your relationship with him. Share your concern that you may have done or not done something that caused a strain in your relationship and you'd like to talk with him about the problem so you can resolve it and move forward. Then ask if he's willing to talk with you so you can work through the issue together. If he says yes, then move ahead with the conversation. If he says no or "I don't know," then ask if he would allow you the opportunity to share your thoughts without his feeling pressure to respond to you.

If he brings up his concerns, be ready to work on them together—one issue at a time. Ask questions to gain insight and clarity. The chapter on coaching (chapter 2) includes effective communication tips along with suggested questions that may help facilitate your discussion. Keep in mind that your goal is to understand your child's perspective. Listen with that intent and respectfully consider his concerns before you respond.

If you are confused, ask your child to help you understand. If he brings up more than one issue, ask that you focus on resolving one at a time. Respect him with your words, your tone of voice, and your body language. If you become uncomfortable or feel attacked, take deep breaths, then communicate that you understand he is concerned and you want to help resolve the problems in a way that is respectful to both of you. Don't let defensiveness cloud your judgment. Look honestly at what you can do to help resolve the conflict.

If your child doesn't bring up the problem but you know there is something you've done that has caused the rift, don't pressure him to identify what's wrong. State that you believe you may have done something to hurt or disappoint him and you want to work together to resolve the concern. Then continue, as long as the door to communication is open.

Once you have listened to your child identify his concerns or expressed your awareness that something you did or didn't do has caused a strain in your relationship, take responsibility without defending yourself or placing blame. "I'm sorry that what I said/did caused problems for you." Or, if you know you were wrong, simply admit, "I was wrong and I'm sorry." Ask for forgiveness. Then give time for him to respond. You may hear a positive reply right away, you may hear a negative response, you may hear him say he'll need to think it over but isn't ready to respond then, or you may hear silence. He may need time to work through his own feelings, and he may want to see how you demonstrate your willingness to take responsibility without shifting blame or setting conditions. Grant him that time and use it as an opportunity to show that you are trying to do your best as a parent to move forward—to contribute the best you can to the relationship.

If Your Child Has Been the One to Cause the Breakdown

A conversation with him needs to be carefully considered in this case. Before you begin to tell him how hurt you are and what he has done to you, work through your emotions as mentioned earlier. Then you can focus more clearly on positive steps to solve the problem and help mend the relationship. Ask yourself what your goal is for the conversation. If it is to point blame, then recognize that you may be successful in telling him what a bad thing he did, but you won't help heal yourself or the relationship. Ask God to help you focus on your goal of reconciliation with your child. The following steps may help guide your conversation:

First, tell your child you'd like to talk with him about something and ask when it would be convenient to have that conversation. Again, timing is crucial. If he will not talk with you, then consider a letter/e-mail or ask if he'd be willing to see someone with you (like a counselor or pastor) to work through a problem.

Begin by communicating your goal. Something like, "I'm concerned about a problem between us and I want to talk with you about it because I would like your help to let it go so we can move beyond it." He needs to understand that your intent is not to attack him but to clear up misunderstandings and work through negative feelings so you can let go of the issue and move on.

Share what happened that hurt you. Avoid sentences that begin with "you." Like, "You made me so mad when . . ." "You hurt my feelings when . . ." Instead, talk about what happened with an emphasis on the problem and not your child's character. For example, "I felt hurt and angry when you didn't follow through like you said you would, because I thought you were disrespecting me and disregarding our agreement. I don't like feeling this way, and I want us to get past this conflict so we can move on."

At that point, your child may take responsibility and ask for forgiveness. He may not. Either way, you can continue with a commitment and a request: "I know I need to forgive what happened and let this go. It would be helpful if you would commit to following through like you agreed to. That will help us both get back on track."

Remember, forgiveness is not conditional on your child's admittance of wrong. It says, "I want to let this go so I can move forward with life. I may carry memories about what happened, but I don't want to carry the pain or the blame." If your child takes responsibility and expresses a desire to move on, then you can talk about ways to get things back in line. If he doesn't, then you'll need to consider how to move forward carefully and prayerfully, with clear, reasonable expectations.

Once you have addressed the offense and agreed to take steps to move past it, do not bring it up again. *Let it go* means just that: Let it go. Agree to release the negative emotions connected with what took place and put the experience in the past as you move forward.

Forgiveness begins with the steps we've considered, and it continues to be reinforced over time. As a memory from the past pops up, a spirit of forgiveness allows us to remind ourselves, "Yes, that happened and I am thankful God has helped us put that behind us so we can move forward." Each time we say that, the memories have less and less power to stir our emotions. Rather than feeling the pain, we experience God's grace in action.

Parents Mending Fences

Sally shared with me her battle with her son's drug use and her struggle to let go and move forward, even though he says he has stopped using:

> Even after drugs became a thing of the past, the constant niggling fear (for his personal safety whether at his own hands—through drug use—or at the hands of others in the "world" of drugs) is hard to shake. Trust has been difficult to regain, and even though the drug abuse is in the past (I know that logically), there is still that grain of mistrust that it's not really over. I believe this has to do with the deep hurt and fear that came with the knowledge he was actually living a life I never thought I'd face with one of my children.

When I asked what made it possible for her to regain that trust in her son, Sally quickly replied, "I think the question is better asked, 'What *makes* it possible?' I think it really is a constant process. I don't know when the day-by-day process will be over in my head and heart even though my son assures me (and has demonstrated) that he is no longer a part of the drug scene."

She went on to explain, "Prayer is key in the healing process. Prayer for my own ability to function without fear and mistrust, and prayer for my son that he will not be tempted back into the life of drugs he left. I think what parents suffer after an experience of a child on drugs is post-traumatic stress disorder. It is so difficult to get over, yet it does get easier with each passing day."

Along with taking steps to rebuild trust as a part of mending fences and moving forward in her relationship with her son, Sally shared, "I needed to learn to enjoy my son again, so the balance of confrontation and hard conversation could begin to shift to healthy and enjoyable conversation and relationship."

I've found the same thing to be true in my relationships with my own children. When we can work on something together, laugh together, share a meal, take a walk, or play a game, our focus shifts to enjoy the present moment. We're reminded of the value in our relationship that we want to protect.

As a young adult man, Barry found his relationship with his parents strained for a time. He shared with me how they have turned a corner and are now enjoying life together more:

> Growing up, I didn't spend much time with my parents. They were both busy between their jobs and their volunteer work. They didn't even see each other much. Oh, they made sure I had whatever I needed in the way of food, clothes, and gas money, things like that. I just didn't see them. I got used to being on my own, so it wasn't a big change when I went off to college. I didn't get homesick or anything. In fact, I didn't call or go home much at all. We didn't fight or anything. We just seemed to live separate lives.
>
> Now that I'm out of school with a job and my own place, we seem to be connecting more. My parents had me over to the

house one afternoon and told me some things happened that got their attention and helped them realize how important time with family really is. We agreed that we can't change the past but we can make more of an effort now to connect with each other. It was a little weird at first because we all had been so independent, but Dad and I have started playing golf and we all eat dinner together on Sundays. We're even talking more openly about things. It's a good start.

My friend Jane shared a powerful lesson God taught her about healing wounds and mending fences from the inside out.

My daughter-in-law is a choleric—some have called her a "closet choleric" as she isn't straightforward, openly opinioned, and demanding like myself.[3] Because she seems indecisive and never raises her voice, our son was totally taken off guard after he realized that he had indeed married a choleric—something he was determined not to do after living with his strong-willed sister and me. Our daughter-in-law is a manipulator behind the scenes. For example, if you ask what they are doing for a holiday, she will give a definite answer. Then after we make plans accordingly, she announces she is planning something else, like taking a trip to see a friend.

There were several years of this, filled with many tears and much frustration. Then one morning I read my devotional for the day, and it happened to be 1 Corinthians 13. The Lord distinctly told me to love my daughter-in-law that way and I told God—no way! She has hurt me too often and I don't want to love her. I prefer to tolerate her. But the Lord would not allow me to leave my quiet time that morning until I had committed to love her. Finally, I dated the Scripture and reluctantly began to listen to the Holy Spirit. He had me begin to send her handwritten notes every week—notes of affirmation and love.

After two months, she finally responded. It was the beginning of learning to love her. At least three times in His Word God tells us that "love covers over a multitude of sins" but little did I realize it would be MY sin the love would be covering. It has been several years now and I will tell you confidently that I love her and appreciate her. Does that mean I don't get frustrated at times? No, it doesn't mean that. But then I get frustrated with everyone I love—myself included.

Our Challenge as Parents

When we take an honest, objective look at our relationships, we'll see that most of us have done at least some things right as parents. Most of our children have as well. Unfortunately, we don't take time often enough to reflect much on those positive acts. The memories that sit on the back burners of our minds, those recollections we have difficulty shaking off, are sometimes filled with pain and disappointment, hurt and regret. They seem to tether us to past mistakes and prevent us from seeing the value in ourselves and in our children.

Focusing on the positives will help us let go of past mistakes, apply grace and forgiveness, and move forward with renewed hope.

Take a moment to step back and look at the big picture as you consider both your acts and your children's. What positive things have you done to help foster a healthy relationship with them? What positive things have they done as well? Consider the small acts that you may take for granted as well as the sacrifices made along the way. It is so important that we look at the complete relationship we have with our children and not just the things that have gone wrong. Focusing on the positives will help us to let go of past mistakes, apply grace and forgiveness, and move forward with renewed hope.

Can we do that on our own? Sometimes, perhaps, but at other times it feels almost impossible. Thankfully, we don't have to rely on our own abilities. We have a loving heavenly Father who gives us grace and forgiveness. And He commands us to forgive others. He also tells us that if we will trust in Him and commit to obeying His desires for us, He will guide our steps and enable us to do all that He requires. Herein lies our hope, our strength, and the opportunity for a fresh start toward a healthy relationship with our children.

On a Personal Note

Are there unresolved hurts from the past that may be interfering with building a healthy relationship with your child, now that he's grown?

If so, what steps will you take to begin the process of mending fences so that you and your child can move forward together?

Consider this passage from the Bible as you ask God to heal your heart and give you the wisdom to know when and how to approach your child to begin that mending process.

> Rejoice in the Lord always. I will say it again: Rejoice! Let your gentleness be evident to all. The Lord is near. Do not be anxious about anything, but in every situation, by prayer and petition, with thanksgiving, present your requests to God. And the peace of God, which transcends all understanding, will guard your hearts and your minds in Christ Jesus. Finally, brothers and sisters, whatever is true, whatever is noble, whatever is right, whatever is pure, whatever is lovely, whatever is admirable—if anything is excellent or praiseworthy—think about such things. Whatever you have learned or received or heard from me, or seen in me—put it into practice. And the God of peace will be with you.
>
> —PHILIPPIANS 4:4–9

Chapter Four

Set Healthy Boundaries— and Follow Through

*"If you would have your son to walk honorably through the
world, you must not attempt to clear the stones from his path,
but teach him to walk firmly over them—not insist upon
leading him by the hand, but let him learn to go alone."*
—ANNE BRONTE, *THE TENANT OF WILDFELL HALL*

Our Need—and Theirs

"Yes, you can go outside to play but you must stay in our yard.
Don't go into the street or over to the neighbor's yard. You know
the rules."

When our children were growing up, our family lived in houses
with fences and grassy areas that clearly defined our property. We
could easily identify where we could plant shrubs without infringing
on our neighbor's property, and our children knew where they could
safely play. Everyone was aware of where our boundaries were, and
things worked well as long as we respected those perimeters. It was
clear and uncomplicated.

Recently my husband and I moved into a different type of

community, and the homes in our area don't have fences. Our yard flows into our neighbors' yards and our backyard connects to a common, shared area. The appearance is neat and uncluttered by wooden or stone borders to separate properties. However, I find myself in a quandary about where I can place things without infringing on someone else's space. My imagination has been working overtime with all sorts of ideas for a relaxing backyard retreat, yet I'm hesitant. I want to create an enjoyable area with a variety of décor, but I don't want to overstep my bounds. So I tend to hold back and keep things close to the house, only to find out later there is more room I can use. Without clear boundaries, I wonder how far can I go before I've crossed the line.

While out and about running errands one afternoon, I was thinking about our younger son who lives near us: *I haven't talked to him in a while. I wonder how he's doing.* It wasn't long before that curiosity began to steer my car toward his house. *I'm so close, with a trunk full of groceries, and I think he's off work today. He probably needs some food; maybe I should just drop by and surprise him with a few things.*

Somehow in the midst of this conversation with myself, I was ignoring the agreement I had previously made with my son that I would respect his privacy and not drop by unannounced. I was also ignoring the understanding we have that he's primarily responsible for his needs. I'm not. But aren't surprise grocery gift deliveries an exception? *I guess I could call him, but I'm right here. Surely it's okay.* I could certainly justify crossing the line, but what would he say? I sat at the end of his road and battled my conflicted heart— helpful vs. intrusive, concerned vs. inconsiderate. What's a mother to do?

Boundaries. They serve an important function in our lives, don't they? While they may seem limiting to some degree, they provide an element of safety along with respect as they identify where we can function without causing problems for ourselves or someone else.

In healthy relationships, boundaries indicate the parameters of each person's privileges and responsibilities—physically, emotionally, financially, and across the scope of our connections with others. They clarify expectations and foster a sense of security and safety that opens the door for trust to develop.

While our children were growing up, our parental responsibility included setting boundaries as we told them where they could go, what they could do, and with whom they could play. We established a bedtime, set rules and consequences, and let them know what to expect from us in terms of our provision and care. We considered their needs and desires as well as our goals and concerns for them. The boundaries we put in place set limitations but also fostered a sense of security.

> We need to set new limits—boundaries— on our actions and expectations to help our children understand the scope of our support as they learn how to manage adult life.

Now that our children have moved into adulthood, our task is to let go of the control over their lives and become supporters and encouragers rather than leaders. They can then take on responsibility for their choices and the consequences—both good and bad—that come with them. Our focus must now center on fostering their independence, responsibility, and personal accountability. As we shift roles, our love and concern continues, but we need to set new limits—boundaries—on our actions and expectations to help our children understand the scope of our support as they learn how to manage adult life.

At the same time, we need to recognize that our children are also setting boundaries about our involvement in their lives. Certainly, it's helpful if this transition takes place gradually and is welcomed by both parents and children. We want that shift and they ultimately do as well. However, the process is not always easy for them or for us.

The Challenge

This idea of our adult children being responsible for their own lives makes sense. Sounds fair. Just let go. Just say no. Easy enough, right? Perhaps in theory that may be true, but parents often struggle in this area of their relationship with their children as they attempt to distinguish between guidance and interference, between helping and enabling.

I once took a series of paint-along classes with some friends. Our collective painting experience was limited to walls, furniture, and our fingernails. But we were eager students with a willing artist to guide us. We set our easels next to hers and watched as she turned a blank canvas into a beautiful landscape. "Just watch me and do what I do," she would tell us. And we did. Or at least we tried.

As we struggled to copy her technique, she would walk around to view our handiwork. "That's not quite right," she would gently whisper when she saw us struggle, so as not to embarrass us. "Let me show you." Then she would take our brush and work her magic on our canvas. We were relieved she fixed our problem so we could go home with something that was fit for the wall and not the trash bin. Week after week we went, we watched, we tried, and she repaired. I sometimes wondered if my painting needed to show her signature as well as mine. I'm not quite sure how much we learned, but we did have a great time.

Then one afternoon we arrived at the studio and were greeted by another artist who was filling in for our instructor. She introduced herself and we began our session. As she worked her artist's magic, we carefully observed and tried to follow along. Then she paused to walk around and watch us in action.

"I can't seem to get this tree to look quite right," I admitted somewhat apologetically, as if she couldn't see the obvious. Assuming she would take my brush and fix the problem, I stepped aside as she came over. She looked at the canvas and responded, "Why don't you try holding your brush at a different angle?" I looked at her and she looked at me with one of those I'm-not-going-to-do-it-for-you smiles.

I tried to follow her suggestion. "It feels a little awkward," I announced, certain she would just step in and help so we could move on. "Try it a few times on your practice canvas. You'll catch on." Then she smiled and walked away. I felt abandoned and frustrated, but I wanted to finish the painting, so I continued working. Funny thing, after practicing a bit, I got the hang of it and went on to complete a painting I was quite proud of. I learned so much from her as we worked together. My confidence soared as she taught and then gave me opportunity to practice. I realized I could best learn by doing it myself—all under her watchful eye and encouraging spirit.

Both teachers cared about me and wanted things to go well. Both showed me what to do and encouraged me to try, but when problems arose, their goals differed. One put my happiness above my education and would quickly come to the rescue when something was difficult. Her approach met immediate needs—my need to solve problems and her desire to make me happy—but it hindered me from learning how to do it myself and fostered my dependency on her. The other teacher pushed me to take charge of solving the problem, at the risk of my frustration, even possible failure. She believed I would learn and grow as an artist best by taking ownership of the challenge.

Little did I know that a few years later I would become a mother and would face having to choose how to guide without interfering, how to help without hindering. Even today, as they are grown men and our roles have shifted, I have to remember my sons are in charge of their choices—and consequences. I am not.

75

My role is to encourage, offer instruction if they ask, then step back and let them decide how they want to paint the canvas of their lives—even when their pictures don't look as I think they should. I can't jump in and grab the brush to paint for them, and I can't be too quick to take the brush if they ask me to. After all, I have my own picture to paint!

Helping or Hindering?

As we learn to navigate this shift in our parenting role and come alongside with guidance, we need to take a look at *enabling,* because that's where parents of adult children sometimes find themselves. While the word *enable* means "to make something possible" or "to provide somebody with the means to do something," in the context of this focus on setting boundaries, enabling refers to doing something for someone that they can do for themselves. In the parent-child relationship, enabling parents attempt to protect their children from the consequences of their behavior. They make it possible for their child to continue actions without dealing with the results, even at the risk of compromising their own beliefs and needs.

The immediate result might be a quick fix to a problem or prevention of difficulties, even pain. However, when parents intervene in this way, their interference—even though well-meaning—enables their adult children to avoid accountability for their behavior. It fosters dependency and hinders both their maturity and a healthy transition into independent living, because the children assume their parents will take care of things and they don't have to be responsible.

This pattern of enabling may take overt forms as parents directly step in and take over, and it may also show up more subtly as parents make decisions for their adult children or help out more than is necessary. Enabling parents do things for adult children such as choosing a college for them; rescuing them every time they experience financial problems; making sure they are on time for work or college; taking care of their laundry and preparing all their meals if they live at home; being on-call to baby-sit whenever asked, no matter what; making decisions for them about career, children, relationships, and housing; and automatically bailing them out of their problems so they avoid consequences.

I don't mean to suggest we should never help our children out. There are situations where that is certainly an appropriate thing to do. The problem with enabling occurs when we take that well-meaning assistance too far, to the point where it moves from supporting to overdoing, from providing needed assistance to doing something they could and should do for themselves.

We say things like, "Maybe you should let me . . ." or, "I want to be sure everything is okay, so I better . . ." Then there's the "I'll take care of it" statement we offer, whether or not they ask for our help, that places us in charge of solving their problem. We either send the message: "I don't think you can do it correctly" or, "You don't have to be responsible. I'll cover for you."

That intrusion hinders their growth and maturity as it fosters low self-esteem, dependency, irresponsibility, and even rebellion in our children. It also stirs resentment, guilt, and frustration within us. Our interference may prevent them from developing the skills and self-confidence that grow through trial and error, through failure and success.

Allison Bottke, author of *Setting Boundaries With Your Adult Children,* cautions:

> As long as we continue to keep enabling our adult children, they will continue to deny they have any problems, since most of their problems are being "solved" by those around them. Only when our adult children are forced to face the consequences of their own actions—their own *choices*—will it finally begin to

sink in how deep their patterns of dependence and avoidance have become.[1]

When we find ourselves struggling internally, thinking we are doing more than we should, we have likely crossed a boundary that we have set up for ourselves. We know what we believe is the "right thing" to do; yet when a need arises, we find ourselves once again stepping in, and our children respond accordingly. Then we complain, "When will they grow up and start doing things for themselves?" Melanie, mother of three adult children, talked about the approach she and her husband take in setting boundaries:

> We've always believed in telling the kids, "You can do any-thing you want, but you need to consider the effects of your choices," and then we try to spell out for them what we see the pitfalls to be. If they still want to go ahead with the choices, we explain what we will or won't do to help them if they get into trouble. Occasionally we've helped anyway (car safety, for example), but they didn't know that going into the situation. We have to let each child be who God created him/her to be, even if that person isn't who we expected our child to become.

There are times when the decision about boundaries between parents and their adult children becomes a point of contention between the parents themselves. One takes a firm restrictive stand and the other, believing the restriction to be too severe, swings to the opposite extreme, resulting in mixed signals for the child and tension between the parents. Carol described the struggle she has with knowing how to set reasonable boundaries and the difficulty in working with her husband to know what is appropriate now that her sons are grown men and learning how to live on their own:

My husband's first instinct (and often his response) is no, and I overcompensate with my yes. When our two boys were little, we could work through it a bit easier because they were good kids and we didn't have many problems. Things just seemed to work out. Now our sons are adults and the issues are more serious. They are struggling with some problems, and I feel bad for them. I know they could use our help, but my husband says they are adults and have to figure it out on their own. I know I need to step back at times and let them deal with things, but I'm afraid if I don't offset my husband's tough stand and try to help, our sons will turn away from us. I feel the distance growing and I just can't let that happen.

One Mother's Experience

Jeanette set some boundaries with one of her daughters that led to her daughter moving away from home for a time:

We asked Carrie (our foster daughter) to move out when she was nineteen because she was staying out late and worrying us. She's very social and just didn't want to play by the rules. For instance, she wasn't particularly interested in doing things with the family anymore. Her friends almost always took precedence. This was hurtful (in particular because we'd taken her into our home several years earlier and had worked so hard to make her feel like family). She just loved being with her friends and didn't care much for hanging out with us.

Also, my husband and I were reaching a point in our lives where we wanted things to slow down. We needed more privacy and space. Her happy-go-lucky, stay-out-till-the-wee-hours-of-the-night schedule just didn't work with us, so we told her something had to change.

She wasn't really prepared to move out and took a real chance (particularly financially) by moving into the apartment with her older sister. She had to take on a second job to cover the extra bills. We encouraged her to be independent and we weren't surprised when we didn't hear much from her (or see her) in the first few months after moving out. We did what we thought was right but it was a difficult time and we all had to work through the consequences—of our choice and hers.

Carrie moved back home after living on her own for a year. It was a tough year for her, and she learned some hard lessons. Money became a major issue and she got behind on bills, but she never came to us to bail her out and she's been working on getting back on her feet. Though she's made mistakes, she's done the right things to make up for them. Talk about a learning curve!

I asked Jeanette how she handled Carrie's request to move back home, responding to her daughter's needs without compromising the boundaries she and her husband had set.

We welcomed her with open arms, for we knew the appropriate lessons had been learned. She was willing to respect our needs and she longed to share time with us more than before. Also, she was at a point where she needed family support when she came back. Her best friend had just been killed in a tragic car accident, and Carrie was going through all of the emotions you might imagine after such a loss. We wanted to set up a plan that would consider her needs as well as ours.

We were clear on our expectations, and she responded respectfully to them. Setting up a budget and sticking to it have been issues for her, but she's getting better all the while. I have no doubt she'll be doing well financially within the year, especially since she's living at home again and doesn't have the big rent payment. We would like her to help with the utility bills but have not set up a definite plan for that as yet.

She still likes to stay out late, but has become more sensitive to our schedules. She's a delightful, happy girl, who can't help it that's she a social butterfly. After a conversation with her, however, she has learned that she must ask me before bringing people home for random "let's just hang out" visits. It always threw me to have people show up unannounced, particularly since I've grown accustomed to an empty house and tend to dress with that in mind. We've drawn much closer since that event, and I can truly say it has caused all of us to become more sensitive to the time we have together.

When we set boundaries and establish limits in terms of the type and degree of support we can give our children, we create an atmosphere that encourages responsibility and accountability for both our children and ourselves. These young adults have the opportunity to develop a spirit of independence as they learn to support themselves. We can continue to offer support, within clearly defined boundaries, resulting in a healthy relationship as our children transition into adulthood.

> When we set boundaries and establish limits . . . we create an atmosphere that encourages responsibility and accountability for both our children and ourselves.

Responding to Needs

We want our children to come to us with their needs and we want to help whenever we can. But we must consider their needs versus their wants, keeping in mind that they may very likely define those two categories differently than we do. We must avoid debating with them, acknowledging that our opinions may differ. Instead we can focus on how we want to assist with *needs* we deem appropriate while not feeling obligated to respond to all the *wants* they may express. To accomplish this task successfully, we must first evaluate each child's unique abilities, characteristics, and situation to decide what is the best way to provide support.

As the mother of adult daughters, sons-in-law, and a growing family of grandchildren, Jeanette has learned that she needs to consider each one individually as she determines how and when to help. She has this advice for parents as we look at setting boundaries regarding helping to meet our children's needs:

> We must remember that they are all individuals. We can't make "across the board," sweeping kinds of decisions. There really are times when we have to take the situation of the child into consideration, particularly if they're dealing with health-related (or sometimes even job-related) circumstances beyond their control. I'm not one of those parents who believes that we should cut them off at eighteen. I have yet to find the chapter and verse for that one. It's an American/societal thing. Biblical families cared for one another throughout their lives, sometimes even living together and growing old together. (I'm not advocating this, just reminding myself that God's plan was always for families to remain in close relationship.)

It's important for us to talk with our children to identify the needs, communicate the goals for both of us, express concerns, and then determine appropriate responses. This process provides a respectful way of developing interdependence between us. As part of this process, we must honestly examine our motives for assisting our children. Growing independence for them means less dependence on us.

On one hand, there may be a sense of relief that the responsibility has shifted. However, there is also a sense of loss as we realize we are not needed in this role. So when a request for help comes, we may see it as a sign that we are, indeed, still needed. As a result, we may respond quickly without full consideration, when perhaps the better form of support would be to step back.

I remember when my sons learned how to ride a bicycle. We began with training wheels attached and my hand firmly gripping the back as they learned how to pedal. Then the day came when it was time to take the extra wheels off. I held the back of the bicycle as the boys struggled to find their balance. "Don't worry, son. I'm holding on." Once I let them get comfortable, I knew I would need to let go so they could take off. So I did. And they did. And at some point they fell. Of course, I rushed over and helped them up, wanting to assure them, "I'm so sorry I let you fall. I'll hold on." I knew, though, that if they were going to learn to ride, I had to let go, even if it meant they would fall down again and again. I knew eventually they'd learn. And they did. I remember watching them ride up and down the street with the biggest smiles. "Look at me, Mommy. I can do it all by myself."

Today my sons are learning how to do other things that bring their own set of challenges, disappointments, and successes. Managing their finances. Cooking. Building successful careers. Maintaining their cars and homes. Strengthening their relationships. Parenting. Planning for their future. Coping with their emotions.

I love it when they call and ask, "Mom, can you help me?" My immediate internal response is, "Of course I will. Whatever you need." I am learning, though, that help doesn't always mean active intervention. There's a time to hold the bicycle, and there's also a time to let go, encourage from the sidelines, cheer their success, and offer empathy if things don't go well. I must pause long enough to understand what's taking place and ask God to clarify my role. I also know there are times when my sons will say, "Thanks for the offer, Mom. I can take care of it myself." I must swallow the disappointment of feeling I'm not needed and recognize the independence that's important for them as adults.

Before We Speak

There are some key steps we can take as we work together to define our roles and establish healthy boundaries for supporting our children. We need to listen and respect our children's perspectives, even if we disagree with them. We can discuss our observations and share opinions—if they are open to receiving them—as long as we maintain honesty and respect, two fundamental building blocks of successful, healthy relationships. We need to remember that our role in the conversation is *not* to judge, control, or lead. It *is* to evaluate the situation and determine the scope of our involvement. Then offer that assistance. Sometimes they want our opinions, other times they just want to know if and how we will help so they'll know what to expect from us and from themselves.

Once we understand the situation, we need to take time out to seek God's guidance as we consider the best response we can give. My husband and I try to allow time whenever possible to talk things through with each other so we can share observations and opinions, then look at options together. Partnering strengthens our relationship and helps us make healthier decisions we can better uphold. Taking time to assess also communicates to our children that we are not letting our emotions rule, but rather trying to discern the best response. Easier said than done at times, I will admit, but important for everyone involved.

Once we've decided that support is warranted and we've determined the assistance we will offer, we need to communicate our intent clearly as we offer our support. If there are conditions to be met, we need to discuss those before we follow through so there is clear understanding and accountability on the part of both parent and child. No surprises. Then, if they accept our offer to help, we can follow through consistently to completion as we agreed we would.

With Choices Come Consequences

Before we communicate the boundaries we are setting with our children, we need to consider the consequences that may take place so we'll be prepared to follow through. Our desires are that our children understand and accept the parameters we have set, and that the results are successful for all of us. Unfortunately, however, that is not always the case, and the consequences are sometimes difficult for us as parents as well as for our children. All too often, our fear of the possible negative consequences prevents us from taking the action we know in our heart is healthy—consequences that may come in our own lives as well as in our children's.

I don't like going to the dentist. Okay, there, I said it, with apologies to those of you who work in the field of dentistry. I like my dentist and her staff, but I don't like the discomfort that comes with some of the reparative work I've had done. So I tend to put appointments off in an attempt to avoid pain, but things only get worse over time. Yet I know if I press through the fear and tackle the discomfort, I'll eventually find relief and healing when the process is over.

While we cannot ignore the possibility of negative outcomes, we must also keep in mind that the end result might be a positive outcome for our children, for ourselves, and for our relationship. We don't know how the future will unfold, so we need to trust in God's guidance and provision, asking Him to calm our fears and grant us wisdom as we set necessary boundaries, prepare for possible consequences, and then move forward.

Tips for Setting Boundaries

We cannot automatically expect our children to take the lead in setting healthy boundaries for our involvement in their lives. Sometimes they do but that is not always the case, especially when they don't want to take the responsibility for the consequences of their choices. Sometimes they want to be in charge of their own lives but lack the confidence to step out and take the steps that come with that ownership. It is up to us as parents to take the lead in establishing, communicating, and upholding healthy boundaries with our adult children as we encourage them to take responsibility for their lives.

Consider the following tips to help you talk with your child about a boundary you desire to establish with him:

- Write down your concerns and the parameters you feel are necessary to set. When you put something in writing, you can review it to be certain you are not giving a strictly emotional response but do have reasoning to support your action. You can read it over to rehearse what you want to share so that you will be able to communicate clearly and maintain your focus on the issue at hand.

- Develop your action plan, communicate a timeline, and consider consequences you may need to enforce if your child does not follow through. Be clear and specific. Don't lecture, debate, attack, or degrade. Speak positively, with the belief that your expectations are reasonable and you have confidence your child can follow through.

- If you are unsure that your expectations are reasonable, talk to someone who can give confidential, wise, objective counsel to help you set healthy boundaries and appropriate consequences.

- Recognize that if your child does not agree with the boundary you are setting, you may get some resistance. Avoid becoming defensive or arguing. Instead, clarify your intent and be prepared to stand firm if you believe your decision is reasonable.

- Consider how to communicate effectively—with love and respect. You may want to review some of the communication tips covered in the chapter on coaching (chapter 2) for suggested phrases to use and those to avoid.

- Keep your ultimate goal in mind: Your intent is not to punish your child, control him, or to make his life miserable. Your desire is to help him take charge of his life and find a healthy, loving way to relate with him that respects both your needs.

Some Helpful Examples

After much prayer and some counseling, Karen and her husband opened the door for their adult son to come back home after struggling on his own for several years. They wanted to give him the opportunity to get back on his feet, but did not want to enable him to continue with some choices they firmly disagreed with. They knew they could not control him but they did not want to do things that appeared to condone lifestyle choices they couldn't support. Here are some of the boundaries they set in place:

He must hold a job, attend church weekly, keep his room and bathroom clean, do his own laundry, and contribute to food expenses. He must agree not to drink alcohol, smoke, or use any illegal drugs in their home, and attend an addiction recovery support group routinely. They expected him to pay his child support on time and honor his visitation schedule with his young daughter. He would need to set up and follow through on a plan to take care of his financial debt and keep Karen and her husband updated on that process. They asked that if he was out in the evening, he would come home at a reasonable hour that they would agree on together so as not to disturb Karen and her husband, who got up very early for work. They also requested that he not have friends over to the house without checking with Karen first. They required that he set goals and a timeline toward living on his own again, without their assistance. If he did not follow through on these boundaries, he would be given a short period of time to make other living arrangements and would need to move out. They told him that their love for him is unconditional, but their support has some specific boundaries.

Karen said that their son—a man in his early thirties—was

resistant to some of their requirements at first. But they believed they were necessary boundaries and stood by them respectfully, firmly, consistently, and lovingly. While they had a somewhat rocky start, six months have passed and things seem to be going much better now. He is working to get back on his feet and independent again.

Karen shared that at times she feels like "the police" and more directive than she'd like to be, but she knows that for the well-being of herself, her marriage, and her son, it is necessary. She knows he could slip back into old destructive patterns at any time. But she is learning day by day to draw strength from the Lord and to remember that God is in control and she is not. She has been learning how to set emotional boundaries in terms of her responsibility for her son's life as well as the physical and financial boundaries she and her husband put in place.

Karen's agreement with her son was verbal; however, some parents find establishing a written arrangement—a contract—helpful, especially in the area of financial assistance. Whether verbal or written, there should be clear expectations with terms and time limits defined before the assistance is given. While this may seem very formal for a "family matter," it sets clearly understood parameters for both parents and adult children to work within. It emphasizes the need, its resolution, and consequences if the agreement is not upheld, with emotions set aside. It respects both parties, allowing parents to provide the support and their child to assume responsibility as an adult for following through.

Jane and her husband have established some workable boundaries with their adult children in the area of financial needs and assistance:

> Neither of our kids have directly asked for money, although they have come right out and told us of a need or desire. We have always told them that if they really get in a bind, please come

to us and we will consider the request. I think both know how conservative we are with our money, and because they respect our values they haven't come with their hand out.

The other side of that coin is that at our own initiative we have been very generous with gifts for our kids and our grandchildren. If, however, we plan and pay for a vacation and invite them, we get to set all the rules and make the decisions. Money talks, I guess you could say. So far, both of the girls (both my daughter and daughter-in-law, who are very strong-minded and controlling at times) have accepted the rules.

In a Crisis

There are situations that call on some parents to set firm boundaries, times when their children are involved in crises. In cases, for example, where there are illegal drugs, illegal activities, or potential harm to someone, parents need to take firm steps to communicate an unwillingness to support those activities in any way. Enabling is a trap parents often fall into during crisis situations out of fear of the consequences their children may face and the inherent desire to protect them from harm. Parents also recognize there may be consequences for themselves as a result of their children's choices, and they want to avoid facing those as well. Because of this, they have difficulty setting firm boundaries that may result in struggles for their children or for themselves.

Parents in situations like these would benefit from consulting with a mental health professional, a minister/counselor at their church, or community resources to understand the dynamics of the crisis for both their adult child and themselves so they can determine how best to respond. They will also benefit from having support to stand with them through the difficult times as they make tough choices and watch consequences unfold.

Most important, parents with an adult child in crisis must realize that God is ultimately in control. They must be willing to turn to Him for guidance and comfort as they trust Him to work in their lives and in the life of their child. While they do so, they must practice loving their child while hating the situation. That involves separating a person from his performance and offering unconditional love, while holding him accountable for the behavior and its consequences. A crisis is often a test of love and a test of faith.

Sowing and Reaping

In their book *Boundaries: When to Say Yes and When to Say No to Take Control of Your Life,* Drs. Henry Cloud and John Townsend caution parents to be aware of the pitfalls of enabling their children and to be mindful of the need to set healthy boundaries regarding involvement in their children's lives. They talk about the law of cause and effect, also known as the law of sowing and reaping, drawing on a passage from the Bible: "Do not be deceived: God cannot be mocked. A man reaps what he sows. Whoever sows to please their flesh, from the flesh will reap destruction; whoever sows to please the Spirit, from the Spirit will reap eternal life" (Galatians 6:7–8). They caution that when we do not set or uphold healthy boundaries in our relationships with our children, we interrupt this law in their lives:

> Rescuing a person from the natural consequences of his behavior enables him to continue in irresponsible behavior . . . the doer is not suffering the consequences; someone else is. Today we call a person who continually rescues another person a codependent. In effect, codependent, boundary-less people "co-sign the note" of life for the irresponsible person. Then they end up paying the bills—physically, emotionally, and spiritually—and the spendthrift continues out of control with no consequences.[2]

The law of sowing and reaping applies to both our children and us, their parents. Each of us is responsible for our behavior—to ourselves, to our family members, and to God. We must consider what we are sowing in the minds and hearts of our children with our words and actions along with the example we are setting for them as they make choices about how to live their own lives. God desires for us to guide our children with love and care, while also tending to ourselves physically, emotionally, and spiritually. He wants us to be good stewards of the talents, blessings, and responsibilities He has given us.

The Other Side of the Coin

We've been talking about the boundaries we set with our children that define how we will be involved in their lives, but we must also consider the boundaries they set with us: the times when they ask us to respect their privacy or limit our involvement, to give them some "space," or perhaps to keep our opinion to ourselves. As parents, we need to be mindful of their requests and not dismiss them too quickly, even if we are uncomfortable with them. We need to talk honestly and respectfully about needs, concerns, expectations, and appropriate boundaries that will be workable for everyone. We need to grant them our respect; and if we find we cannot follow through, we need to let them know our reasoning.

Their desire to set boundaries with us becomes apparent, for example, as we interact with their friends, their spouses and children, their in-laws, and co-workers. It comes into play often when they have their own living space and ask that we not show up without calling first. It is also becoming an increasing issue with respect to social networking.

Facebook is a prime example of a means of connecting with others that we need to carefully consider. It's quick. It's simple. It's also public. A friend of mine, who is the mother of adult daughters, told me that her mother (their grandmother) is following the girls on Facebook and calls her frequently to let her know what they are saying on their own pages and even on the pages of their friends. My friend shared that while she is also on Facebook, she is trying to respect her daughters and doesn't make any written comments that could be deemed interfering, imposing, or embarrassing, and doesn't spy to see what they are saying to others. She and her daughters discussed how they all want to handle this new means of communication without feeling like anyone is snooping or infringing. They have set some boundaries that work for all of them.

Another boundary we need to respect concerns the relationship our children can have with each other and with their sisters- or brothers-in-law. We can encourage them to spend time together, time that doesn't necessarily involve us, to cultivate their relationships. That means we must avoid feeling resentful or left out if they plan events that don't include us. It's important for families to find a balance as they plan time to share together, allowing opportunity to cultivate the various relationships that weave together to form the family unit.

> Honesty, respect, understanding, consistency, and love are essential keys to setting boundaries that will encourage the development of healthy relationships.

There may be times when even the most loving siblings disagree, and we must be careful as parents to avoid stepping into the middle of those conflicts or responding with one of two extremes. If one (or all) come to you complaining, don't dismiss them too abruptly with, "I don't want to hear about it. I'm not getting involved." That may come across as a lack of concern or compassion on your part. On the other hand, don't get drawn into the issues through lengthy, detailed conversations or feel forced to take sides or resolve their conflict. Instead, acknowledge that you know there is a problem (without getting into the details of a he said/she said dialogue). Let your children know you love and respect each one, whether or not you agree. Encourage them to work through their differences to find a resolution and pray for them.

Honesty, respect, understanding, consistency, and love are essential keys to setting boundaries that will encourage the development of healthy relationships. When we sow these seeds, we will reap the joy of knowing we are doing all we can to foster the best relationships we can have within our families.

On a Personal Note

Are there boundaries you need to set with an adult child that will help build a healthy relationship with him by clarifying the parameters of your support while still allowing him to take responsibility for his own life?

What may make this task difficult for you?

What will help you accomplish this step?

Who can support you as you set the needed boundaries?

As you communicate the boundaries you believe need to be set in place, remember:

- Listen first—to your child and to your own heart.

- Ask the Lord for wisdom to identify the true needs and your role.

- Consider how you can help.

- Speak the truth in love.

- Be specific about the kind of support you can give and the conditions that come with that support.

- Clarify your position if those conditions are not met.

- Fulfill your part of the agreement.

- Accept the consequences.

- Hold on to your trust in God's guidance for your child and for yourself.

Chapter Five

Handle Disappointments With Care

"Making the decision to have a child is momentous—it is to decide forever to have your heart go walking around outside your body."
—Elizabeth Stone, author and historian

We baby boomers grew up in a society that expected a lot of us. We had a mandate from our parents, our teachers, even ourselves to be all we could be: to achieve the utmost and to make wise choices about our careers, our finances, and our marriages—to become upstanding individuals. We believed that if we did those things, life would be great for us, perhaps even better than it was for our parents.

Then as we began to have children of our own, we developed a similar set of expectations for them and coupled that dream with a commitment to be the very best parents. Perfect parents. If we read the right parenting books, if we provided the proper education and social activities, if we took our children to church, if we provided all they needed and pushed them to succeed, they would grow up to be healthy adults who would make the right choices for their lives. And as we imagined from all the fairy-tales we read as children, we would all live "happily ever after."

Then our dreams got a reality check. Perhaps our expectations—for ourselves and our children—were not quite realistic, given how our lives have unfolded. While they may be making healthy, wise, successful choices as adults, our children don't always follow *our* plans for their lives or make choices we find agreeable. And sometimes they make mistakes.

As they grew up, we encouraged them to be independent and think for themselves. But now that they are doing so, some of their choices surprise us—sometimes with pleasure and sometimes with pain. Their decisions may reflect subtle differences in styles or perspectives, while other choices may have a major impact on their lives and perhaps on ours as well.

No matter what we teach our children as we raise them and how well we try to direct them down what we believe to be the right path for them, there are times they make choices that disappoint us, concern us, even break our hearts. We watch as they move into adulthood, sometimes rebelling against our suggestions and making decisions we believe are detrimental. They may wander off from everything we taught them, everything we stand for and believe in. Prodigals. We find ourselves on the sidelines, watching from afar, but unable to stop them from what we believe to be harmful choices.

We know, in theory, that their choices and the consequences that follow are not ours to deal with directly, but it's difficult to simply step back and say, "Oh well, it's not my problem." Our hearts break when we see our children choose something we believe will hinder their lives, something harmful, or something that clashes with the very values we tried to instill in them when they were young.

Our fears stir along with our concerns and even a sense of guilt, perhaps, that we didn't do enough to keep them on the right path. Now that we've hit midlife, we find ourselves evaluating many of our own choices, particularly when it comes to parenting. And if we're not careful, we may connect our identity somewhat with the kind of adults our children have become. We look at their successes and failures as measures of our own.

When we agree with their choices, we cheer them on with pride and a sense of relief that life is going just the way we planned for them. In those moments we feel we did our parenting job well. However, when they make decisions that disappoint us, we must sort through a barrage of emotions while maintaining a meaningful connection with our children. All while attempting to remind ourselves that we're trying to be the best parents we can be. Dr. Jane Adams, author of *When Our Grown Kids Disappoint Us*, describes the struggle we have during those disappointing times as our emotions whirl.

> **When they make decisions that disappoint us, we must sort through a barrage of emotions while maintaining a meaningful connection with our children.**

> Our feelings often contain elements of both fear and anger, especially when our grown kids' lifestyles, values, and interest in being in relationship with us are very different from ours. Even while recognizing their right to live and behave as they choose, it's possible to feel worried, disappointed, betrayed, and abandoned; what's really impossible is *not* feeling any of those emotions.[1]

Moms Share Their Stories

Margaret devoted her life to raising her son and trying to instill in him godly values. Once he ventured out on his own as an adult, she began to encounter disappointments as she watched him make choices that brought difficult consequences:

> Handling disappointments has, somewhat, become a way of life for me, or so it seems. Quite frankly, I never dreamed I

would experience such intense pain with the choices of my son. Particularly the life-changing choice he made with a premarital pregnancy in his junior year of college. My response was varied depending on the day of the week. I experienced floods of anger, guilt (Where had I gone wrong in teaching him about poor choices?), fear, embarrassment, and despair. Somehow, I managed to carry the heaviness of my heart while carrying on with life's daily activities, but it wasn't easy. For a long time as I woke up each morning, my heart would hit bottom as the thoughts of his situation began to stir. Nothing is so difficult as to carry around a heavy heart. The emotions were overwhelming and I just wanted to hide.

Finally I realized I had to get a grip on things before I lost my relationship with him, so I took a deep breath and began to face the facts. I chose a small network of friends to open up to and as I did so, I began to see that I wasn't the only one experiencing this kind of situation. I realized things could be much worse than they were. My friends and my relationship with God comforted me as I drew closer to Him. There is no advice that I can give to heal pain. That is something that God and time will do.

Margaret's son has now taken responsibility for his life and the life of his new child. He's married, holding a steady job, and attending church with his young family. God is bringing healing to Margaret and her son as they both learn how to move forward. That's not to say he hasn't made other choices that concern her, but she's learning how to step back a bit emotionally and deal with disappointments.

There are times when parents and their adult children can work through the disappointments, reconcile, and move forward together. However, that positive ending doesn't always occur. Choices have consequences that sometimes last a lifetime, and parents must work through their grief and learn how to accept what has taken place so they can move on with their own lives. Charlotte shares her story here:

My son was an artist. His drawings looked professional and he'd almost gotten his certification in Graphic Design. He'd been in/out of jail and prison for selling and using drugs, but had been clean for a while until he got caught smoking marijuana on campus. His education ended short of his goal. Since he did have some printing experience, he applied for and landed a job with a Christian publishing company in their print shop. I don't think they knew about his former drug use. I celebrated and thanked God for the news.

He worked for the company for several months, and I rejoiced. During this period of his life, he did better than most others. I encouraged him at every turn and praised his efforts on the job.

Then he decided to change jobs. He felt he couldn't make enough money, so he went to work for a tattoo parlor. That's the excuse he gave me, but I knew better because tattoos were part of his drug past. How I hated to see him immerse himself again in this culture. I begged him to try and get his job back at the publishing company. I had hoped he'd settle down and make something of his life. Sure enough, he became entangled again in the drug culture, and his life went downhill from there.

I asked Charlotte how she coped with such pain, knowing her son (now deceased) continued to walk such a destructive path. "What kept you going?"

"All I could do was try to be the best parent I could be. I set boundaries for his benefit and mine and determined not to pamper his every whim. I tried to set a good example myself and cautioned him to avoid places that lead to destruction. I encouraged him in faith and in wholesome activities. Most of all, I knew I must pray for him without ceasing."

"Charlotte, what advice would you give other parents whose adult children are making choices that are unhealthy?"

"If you find these things I tried do not deter their bad choices, there's nothing more you can do except to release them to the Lord and let them live life in the manner they choose. Don't nag them. My wise husband has often said, 'Don't waste your breath.' Adopt the Serenity Prayer as a motto."

When our children make choices that disappoint us, we can easily get caught up in our own emotions, and the fallout can have a negative impact on our lives, physically, emotionally, in our relationships, and even spiritually. Charlotte has some words of caution for parents who struggle to cope:

> Don't let your wayward child or children rule your life by their disappointing choices. Go on with your life. Don't carry their weight on your shoulders. Live your life in the way God would have you live it. Develop your own interests and friends. You might even join a support group of others with children who make bad choices. I called mine The Sorry Son Club. Keep a sense of humor. Don't get drawn into your child's lifestyle in a way that will compromise your values or your boundaries. Stand up for what you believe. Point is, don't let your children's choices kill you, change your way of living your life, or make your life miserable. Love them, but don't try to live their life or let them ruin yours. And again, pray without ceasing. I wish I could say my son turned his life around. He died from cirrhosis of the liver and other drug- and alcohol-related diseases at the age of thirty-five. Oh, the pain. I wondered what I did wrong. I knew I didn't do everything right, but no parent does. Children don't come with an instruction book.
>
> The words of the pastor who performed his funeral helped me the most. "Charlotte, God was the perfect parent, but His children didn't listen to Him either."

Both Margaret and Charlotte learned important lessons about how to cope when children disappoint. The choices they made in how to respond to their children while also taking care of themselves may serve as a guide when you face your own disappointing times.

Here are some tips I have recommended to clients, and I find them helpful personally as I work through disappointing times in my own life:

- Acknowledge your feelings. Don't suppress them. Don't minimize them. Don't exaggerate them. Find safe ways to vent through journaling, talking, exercising, praying, and other expressive avenues.

- Don't withdraw from others and become reclusive.

- Find a safe, confidential, objective person to support you as you work through your emotions and determine how to respond.

- Don't lash out to punish your child or try to make him feel guilty or ashamed because he hasn't met your expectations.

- Try to understand why your child made the choices he did.

- Look for an open door to talk to him. Express your concerns without attacking. Speak the truth in love as you reference facts and logic rather than your hurt or disappointment. Avoid "You made me feel. . . ." Instead, share something like, "I'm concerned about the choice you made and I'm trying to understand it, accept it, and move beyond it."

- Suggest possible changes if appropriate. "I'd like you to think about . . ." "I'm asking you to consider . . ."

- Accept that your child will not always make the choices you would like him to make. You don't have to like it, but you do need to accept that reality.

- Separate your identity from your child's choices. They are not your successes, nor are they your failures. Do the best you can to encourage your child, but realize he has a free will to decide for himself how he will live his life.

- Do all you can to support the aspects of your relationship that *are* working.

- Love your child unconditionally by separating your love for him from your approval or disapproval of his choices. And let him know you are doing so.

- Pray. Ask God for healing for you. Ask Him to grant you the ability to let go of your disappointment, to accept your child's independence, and to move forward toward the best relationship possible. Pray for wisdom for your child to make wise life choices and for open doors to share God's love with him.

- As you focus on healing, find avenues to minister to others, to shift your focus away from your own struggles and bring good out of the pain you have worked through.

When We Disappoint Our Children

As much as we try to make the right choices ourselves and do things that will be pleasing in the eyes of our children, we don't always garner their approval. It's difficult when you know your child is upset with you, when they don't agree with your life choices, or when they tell you that you've let them down. While you might believe firmly that your actions have been the right ones, it's still hard to deal with their anger, hurt, and disapproval.

When they were little children, we told them *no* with the belief that they'd be upset for a bit but would get over their anger and we'd soon hear, "I love you, Mommy." Sometimes we'd explain our actions to them, other times we'd tell them they would have to trust us and respect our decisions, even when they didn't understand.

Now that they're adults, the children we've raised to be independent thinkers are telling us what they think, letting us know with their words and actions—sometimes through their silence and withdrawal—when they don't like the choices we are making. When they're disappointed in us, we must learn how to respond in a way that's respectful and understanding, while not compromising our own beliefs. Teri and her husband divorced when her daughter Jill was very young. Jill's sadness over that loss continues to impact their mother/daughter relationship, even though Jill is now an adult and married with children of her own. Teri shares her struggle here:

As all parents learn, parenting doesn't end when the children are grown and move on to careers, their own families, and their own choices. Knowing when parenting requires biting your tongue or sharing your thoughts can be a difficult challenge. We've always told our children that we love them even if we don't like their choices. Often, I didn't think they believed us. Our oldest daughter—after over twenty-five years—still blames me for the divorce from her father. Her anger flares, often over inappropriate subjects, and she discounts or makes disparaging comments when I offer ideas or advice regarding issues with her children.

I used to pursue her responses to try to learn why she was so belligerent over seemingly innocuous subjects. Her response is still to become angry and tell me not to tell her how to raise her kids, I had my child-raising time, now it's her time with her kids, and she can take care of them without me.

Early on, I would be terribly hurt, confused, and become angry, feeling I didn't deserve such treatment. I've learned, over many years, to give her more emotional space, stay nonthreatening with minimal advice, and not take to heart the hurtful things she says. This way, our relationship, though not close, stays open and cordial. I never fail to let her know I love her and that I'm sorry I can't help her. I also make sure she knows I'll be there for her if she needs me. Period. Very infrequently does she say she loves me, but I'm learning to be okay with that.

As a mother, some of my greatest pleasure has come when I do something that brings a thumbs-up from one of my sons. Their smile of approval is priceless. Some of my deepest hurt has come when one of them lets me know he is disappointed in a choice I've made. Their happiness is important. Yet more important, I need to make the best life choices I can make, no matter how tough those decisions might be—even when my children disagree with me. We share many things in common, but we also have some different viewpoints, and there are times when our differences clash, leading to disappointments. And sometimes I make mistakes.

If you find yourself making choices that bring disappointment to your children, consider these steps to help you work through the conflict with them:

- Let them express their disappointment as long as they do so in a respectful way. Acknowledge you've heard them by saying something like, "I understand you're upset with my choice, and I'm sorry we see things differently."

- Examine your actions to be certain the choices you made were the right ones. Remind yourself why you made the choices you did.

- Share information if they are open to listening, but avoid taking a defensive stand with them. If they don't want to hear your reasoning at that time, don't push. Let them know the door is open if they want to talk later on.

- If you find, in retrospect, that you should have made a different choice, take the needed steps to correct your course and let them know what you've done and why.

- Maintain other aspects of your relationship with your child in as positive a manner as you can. Don't go overboard to compensate, just continue as you routinely do.

- Ask God to grant each of you understanding, patience, and acceptance, and to let your love for each other heal your disappointments.

- Give time for healing, for everyone.

- Get professional help if you have difficulty working through your own emotions, or if you and your child are at an impasse (and you both are willing to have someone help you work through the conflict).

- One additional thing I find helpful is to focus on other aspects of my life to be sure my mind doesn't become consumed with my child's feelings.

When Life Disappoints

As parents, we try our best to protect our children from life's difficulties. However, we know that's not always possible. Dreams sometimes go unfulfilled. Relationships fall apart. Opportunities pass them by. People let them down. Educational goals sometimes must be set aside. Financial losses set them back. Physical illness interrupts plans. Grief and loss, in many different forms, hinder their ability to meet their own expectations, and we face our own disappointments when life doesn't go as we wish it would—for ourselves or for our children.

> It's through life's disappointments that we sometimes learn life's most powerful lessons.

When life brings disappointment, we can (hopefully) work through the grief, pick ourselves up and move forward. When our children face disappointment, our desire is to shield them, to hurry them through the experience, or to fix it for them. But we can't. And even if we could, we shouldn't. It's through life's disappointments that we sometimes learn life's most powerful lessons about patience, forgiveness, and acceptance—about coping with pain and learning to pick ourselves up to begin again. Most important, we learn how to draw close to God, to feel His arms of comfort and healing as He embraces us with His love.

When those times come for our children, we must recognize that there will be a sense of grief and loss on some level. They may experience some pain as they face disappointments, and we, as loving parents, will hurt for them. We can help them work through this process by understanding the journey of grief and allowing time for emotions to process and healing to take place.

An important place to begin is to remind ourselves that we cannot fix this for them. We are not their healer, God is. What we *can* do is support them as they work through it. We can let them know we believe in them and are confident they will work through their disappointments and move forward with life. We need to offer empathy—to come alongside them with our love and support. But ultimately, it's their journey.

Think about a time when you faced a disappointment. Who came to your side with support? A friend? A spouse? A minister? What was helpful as you struggled to work through your emotions? What brought you comfort? What helped you own and safely express your feelings so you could release them and move ahead? Talking to someone you trust? Doing something physical as a release? Journaling? Praying?

Words of encouragement like these may have opened the door to work through your own past disappointments, and they may be helpful support to your children as they deal with their own:

- "I know this is hard for you. I also believe, in time, you'll work it through."

- "I have confidence in you and I know you'll get to the other side of this."

- "I care about you and I'm here for you."

- "Let me know how I can support you through this."

- "If you want to talk about it, I'm here to listen."

- "You have my love and prayer support."

Remember when your child was a toddler, learning how to do things? You often stepped in with, "Let me help you," only to hear his determined reply, "I do it myself, Mommy." We knew that, if possible, we needed to step back and give him the time and space to learn how to work it through. As he grew up, so did his spirit of independence: "Mom, I can take care of it. I don't need you to get involved. I'll be okay."

Then there were those times we heard that little voice say, "Help me, Mommy. I can't do it." We rushed in to see if he did need help or if the best help we could give was to step back, give a word of encouragement, and allow time for him to figure it out on his own. "Come on, son. You can do it. Don't give up. You'll figure it out."

Timing is important as we consider how to share words of instruction on how to assess a situation and let go of hurts. We must listen first and let our child know we are there to support, not to direct or judge. You might want to refer back to some of the suggested phrases to help facilitate discussion, included in chapter 2, on coaching. Sometimes the best gift we can give someone who is grieving a loss is our silent presence. Listening without interruption, without judgment, without dismissing the situation too quickly, and without trying to solve things. Simply to be present—physically, emotionally, and prayerfully.

When our children face life's disappointments, they benefit by knowing we are on the sidelines giving our love and prayer support, understanding their struggles to the best of our ability, and believing they can and will work things through. These gifts will help equip them to get through their disappointments and determine how best to move forward. We can pray that God will give them wisdom as they make crucial choices, knowing His plan for them may not be the same as ours but will be what is best for them. After all, they are His children, and He reminds us in His Word: "For I know the plans I have for you," declares the Lord, "plans to prosper you and not to harm you, plans to give you hope and a future" (Jeremiah 29:11).

When challenges come, I want to know what's happening, what to expect, and the plan for solving the problems. The unknown is not a comfortable place for me. Yet so often in my life, things have happened and God has moved in ways that baffle my mind and call on me to let go of my need for understanding and place my faith in Him to work things through according to His plans.

> When our children face life's disappointments, they benefit by knowing we are on the sidelines giving our love and prayer support, understanding their struggles to the best of our ability, and believing they can and will work things through.

God tells us we will not always understand what He is doing in the life of our children or in our own lives. We must trust in His love and His guidance, even when we don't understand. "For my thoughts are not your thoughts, neither are your ways my ways," declares the Lord. "As the heavens are higher than the earth, so are my ways higher than your ways and my thoughts than your thoughts" (Isaiah 55:8–9).

Our role as their earthly parents is to encourage our children to seek His design for their lives, to make choices that will honor Him, and to trust that He will guide their steps. Personally, we must also put our faith in God, believing He loves our children and will guide their lives as they look to Him. Then we can gently, confidently remind them of His love for them and His willingness to see them through whatever happens.

What About Our Own Disappointments in Life?

I want to say just a brief word about how we handle our own lives and the impact this has on our children. Life doesn't always go as we plan either, and we must pay attention to how we deal with our own disappointments. Our children love us and want to support us through difficult times. We must be careful how we manage their concern and our desire or need for support.

One extreme is to hide things from them and not let them know we're struggling. "I'm fine. Everything's great." If they are close to us, they recognize signs that all is not well. They either worry about us, perhaps more than necessary, or they resent that we won't share our lives with them, thinking we are shutting them out. On the other extreme, we may share too much information, thus worrying them and prompting them to feel responsible to solve our problems.

It's healthy to have an open relationship with our children and share our disappointments, as long as we are careful and respectful about what we share. We should also let them know we are confident we can work through our concerns and will seek help from them or someone else if needed. It will be helpful to let them know how they can support us. When they see us work through our own disappointments, they have an example of how God carries us through whatever challenges life brings—a powerful lesson for our children and a continual growing place for us.

Out of the Ashes of Pain

Deborah Dunn, licensed marriage and family therapist, author, and mother of adult children, shared with me her story of how God carried her through disappointing times with family members and how He wove her pain into ministry that now supports others facing relationship challenges:

Sometimes the most difficult grief to bear is that which comes from watching our children continue down a path of self-destruction, not just once, but over and over again.

For many years I tried to help my young brother come clean from alcohol abuse and drugs, but in 1990 (at the age of twenty-six), just when we thought he had turned a corner, he got up in the middle of the night, walked into his bedroom, and put a gun to his head.

My own children have not been immune from making some really serious life mistakes, particularly where romance and marriage was concerned. Not only did I have to deal with these issues as a very loving parent, but as a relationship therapist as well.

How do we cope with the pain, the anger, the shame of it all, and especially the fear? After all, as much as we try to pray and stay positive, all we have to do is pick up the papers and read that we are not always guaranteed that happy ending. What do we do when we don't know what to do anymore?

Besides prayer, I threw myself into writing, mastering my craft, and learning new skills as a therapist. I became deeply involved in community disaster education. Much to my surprise, journaling turned into a book contract, something I would never have expected. I founded a nonprofit and travel all over the world teaching community disaster education and trauma mental health, as well as doing corporate crisis intervention.

The struggle with my children went on for almost seven years. But my thirty-five-year-old son is now a devout Christian, and I see that his struggles, though painful, were the very thing that took him to his knees before the Lord. My daughter is now a strong young woman who is fearless and travels all over the world herself as a professional kayaker. Of course, I wasn't able to help my brother, but even that terrible loss has reaped some good. I doubt seriously that without that experience I would be a therapist at all. And being a therapist has helped me reach out to thousands of people with my message of hope and healing, especially those with broken relationships.

Disappointments are a part of life. As we build our relationship with our children—now that they're adults—we must learn how to effectively manage our own disappointing times and encourage our children to find healthy ways to work through their own. We need *understanding* about what we are experiencing, *wisdom* to know how to work through our emotions so we can let go and move forward, and *time* to accomplish those things. These tools of healing will help us move through disappointing times so we can step forward and experience life to its fullest. Above all, comes God's intervention in our lives as He lovingly uses the ashes of our disappointments to restore joy to our lives and bring honor and glory to Him. *Jehovah Rapha—the Lord Our Healer.* Deborah expressed that guiding principle so well: "It all comes down to one thing: We must allow God to take our pain, anger, and fear and use it in His kingdom. That is the best therapy of all!"

> We need *understanding* about what we are experiencing, *wisdom* to know how to work through our emotions so we can let go and move forward, and *time* to accomplish those things.

On a Personal Note

What disappointments are you currently facing? What about those of your adult child?

What steps can you take to work through your own grief or support your child as he deals with his own?

Reflect on the following Scriptures as you seek God's guidance and encouragement for you and for your child:

We are hard pressed on every side, but not crushed; perplexed, but not in despair; persecuted, but not abandoned; struck down, but not destroyed. . . . Therefore we do not lose heart. Though outwardly we are wasting away, yet inwardly we are being renewed day by day.

—2 CORINTHIANS 4:8–9, 16

Praise be to the God and Father of our Lord Jesus Christ, the Father of compassion and the God of all comfort, who comforts us in all our troubles, so that we can comfort those in any trouble with the comfort we ourselves receive from God.

—2 CORINTHIANS 1:3–4

Chapter Six

Make Room for New Branches
on the Family Tree

*"Your family and your love must be cultivated like a garden.
Time, effort, and imagination must be summoned constantly to
keep any relationship flourishing and growing."*
—JIM ROHN, ENTREPRENEUR AND MOTIVATIONAL SPEAKER

I had many dreams and goals for my children as they were growing up. Their education and careers, their relationships and achievements, their spiritual growth, even thoughts about marriage for them. Nothing wrong with dreaming. Parents envision all kinds of scenarios for how their children's lives will flow. After all, we know our children and we know what's best for them, don't we?

Then one day we turn around to see that the pages on the calendar have flown by and our children are now adults, dreaming their own dreams and charting their own life course. We watch as they consider adding branches to the family tree (or not) of their own choosing and in their own timing. They may or may not ask our opinions, though ultimately they are making decisions that will impact their lives and ours as well. What is our best response? To respect their independence, to give advice carefully (when asked), to accept (not to be confused with *like*) their choices, and to respond in a way that will foster a healthy adult-to-adult relationship with them, and a partner if they choose one.

If they remain single, we must be careful not to pressure them or imply that their life is incomplete. Instead, we need to encourage them to seek God's direction for their lives and to find peace and joy in knowing they are following His plan for them. If they do choose to invite a marriage partner to share life with them and become part of the family, we must be ready to support them to the best of our ability and make room on the family tree for a son- or daughter-in-law, and perhaps for grandchildren as well. As we prepare to graft on a new branch, we must also realize that the picture will shift a bit and the tree will take on a new look.

> As we prepare to graft on a new branch, we must also realize that the picture will shift a bit and the tree will take on a new look.

Leaving and Cleaving

Jill was excited when her son Bart married a young woman he met at college. Jill and her husband, Tom, had an open, loving relationship with each other and with their children, so they looked forward to that connection growing stronger as Bart invited Sara into their family. Jill shared with me that she soon began to realize how the concept of leaving and cleaving would impact her relationship with her son:

> I guess moms need to come to the realization that they aren't their son's number one girl anymore. I know he still loves me, but now another woman has captured his heart in a new way. It's just as God intended, but if I'm honest, it's hard for me at times and makes me feel as if he doesn't need me anymore. There have been occasions, for example, when we made plans with Bart

and Sara, and then she changed her mind. I try really hard to not make him pick sides. His new wife, and their marriage, needs to be his top priority, and he needs to learn when and how to speak up—to his wife and to his parents. This leaving and cleaving is an adjustment for all of us. I think my husband will experience that same feeling when our daughter falls in love.

We know if our children choose to marry, God intends for them to make their marriage the second most important relationship in their lives, after their relationship with Him. He communicated His intent for the marriage relationship when He joined Adam and Eve together: "That is why a man leaves his father and mother and is united to his wife, and they become one flesh" (Genesis 2:24).

We hear that Scripture often shared in wedding ceremonies, but do we communicate to our children—through our words and actions—that our loving and supportive relationship with them will change now that they have a partner to share the responsibilities and challenges of life? That shift must take place from both directions as our children learn to look to their spouses as their primary support and guide—to come together as one. Our role is to acknowledge and support that shift by stepping back a bit (not in our love but in our direct involvement) as we encourage the couple to develop their partnership.

A Word About Wedding Plans

A wedding is a significant time in the life of our children, and we have the opportunity to come alongside them with our encouragement and support, and hopefully our blessing. While it's a time to celebrate a special addition to our family and a milestone in our parenting journey, it is first and foremost our children's celebration. And we need to honor it as such.

I've been involved in numerous weddings through the years,

helping brides and grooms with the music and flowers and coordinating various elements to help transform their dreams into memorable times of celebration. As I helped them with their planning, I wondered if I would someday be a mother-of-the-groom and be part of all the grand festivities I had planned for others. What flowers would she choose? What music would they want? Would it be a large church or a small chapel? How formal would I dress? How would we celebrate with family and friends? Would I be part of the planning and preparation?

Then my older son and his fiancée shared that they wanted an intimate wedding on a beach with simply their close family members and best friends present. We understood their rationale and agreed completely. I knew it would be a beautiful time of celebration wrapped in love. It would just be different than I had expected. The couple did include us in their planning, and God blessed us all as we shared a wonderful time together. Then we had the opportunity later on to celebrate with family, friends, and the new couple. As I look back, I know things unfolded just as they needed to and I wouldn't change a thing.

When our children decide to marry, they need to be in charge of the planning and their wishes need to be the top priority. Ceremonies and celebrations have taken many different approaches from when we married years ago, and we need to understand that our children's tastes and desires may be different from ours. We must talk with them early on about any assistance they would like from us, and we need to communicate clearly what we can offer in the way of time, finances, and participation. If we have limitations or concerns, we need to communicate those respectfully and clearly so they can determine how to move forward with their plans. It's also important to respect the role of other parents involved and do all we can to foster a cordial relationship with them as we come together to celebrate the marriage of our children.

What If We Don't Approve?

While our children are adults and responsible for their choices, there are times when we have concerns—about their wedding plans or the timing of their marriage—and feel the need to express them. There may be concerns about adjustment challenges as they begin to share life together, or perhaps concerns about their choice of a spouse. For example, I've counseled parents who struggled greatly when their children opted to marry someone of a different culture, background, or faith. Some have had to come to terms with their child's choice to share life with a live-in partner without marrying. I've also worked with parents who struggled with their children's decision to live a homosexual lifestyle with a same-sex partner.

Some parents can find a place of acceptance by realizing that their adult children have to make up their own minds about their beliefs and choices. Others struggle with shock, confusion, disagreement, disappointment, hurt, even feelings of failure and shame. Parents who have difficulty finding a place of resolution often benefit from the support and guidance of a counselor, one who can help them sort through their emotions and determine how best to move forward in a way that is honest, respectful, and loving.

It's especially difficult if our children make relationship choices we don't agree with, especially those that clash with our values or shatter dreams and expectations we had for them. To avoid slamming the door on our relationships with them, we must manage our concerns carefully and remember there is a time to speak and a time to keep silent.

It's important for us to clarify whether our concerns are about our preferences or about problem areas that could be harmful to our children. Most often, we need to accept that we have different opinions, and keep our preferences to ourselves unless asked. We must acknowledge (to ourselves and to our children) that they are adults and responsible for their own choices.

If we have concerns we feel we must share with our child, particularly with regard to their physical, emotional, or financial safety and well-being, we need to first bathe those concerns in prayer, and then speak with respect and love, avoiding judgment. Oftentimes, asking questions will allow our child the opportunity to consider issues without feeling we are trying to control or condemn. Examples that express some of the concerns I hear parents address would be:

- "You come from different life experiences. I'm wondering if you are finding some common ground, and how you will manage conflicts that may arise as a result of the differences."

- "If you choose a same-sex partner, have you considered how you will manage the challenges that may come in your relationships with family, friends, or colleagues, as well as in other aspects of your lives?"

- "You seem to have strong opinions about ____. Do you share the same beliefs? Are you finding ways to accept and work with those who differ?"

- "Have you talked about your individual goals and how (or if) they blend? Have you set shared goals as well?"

- "Have you discussed how you will handle (finances, children, religion, sex, careers, household responsibilities, holidays, and celebrations)?"

- "Are you comfortable with the way you have worked through conflicts and disappointments?"

- "Have you both considered each of your strengths and weaknesses? Can you accept (and live with) both?"

- "Honesty, respect, safety, and trust are vital to a healthy relationship. Are you confident these things are in place, and do you see them in action?"

There are a number of coaching questions in chapter 2 (if they are open to that conversation) that may be helpful as you prompt your child and his/her mate to consider the steps they are taking together.

Rhonda and her husband were concerned when their son told them he wanted to marry. She shares her story here about how they expressed their concern and what took place:

> When my son called to tell me he'd met a special girl, I could tell from his voice that she was going to be the one. I was concerned that they were going too fast when they were engaged after only eight months and planned on getting married after only a year. I tried to tell them they should take their time, but my son's fiancée took that as my not liking her, and it upset him.
>
> The conversation ended, but my concern didn't. I wanted each of them to live on their own for a period of time before they got married so they could learn how to take care of themselves and manage finances without feeling the need to depend on someone else to be okay. My son's wife was going from "Daddy's girl" and Daddy paying everything to married and on a strict budget, living off one salary while finishing school. She told me once that she had never been poor before, so I was concerned about how they would deal with the financial challenges that would come, especially in the first few years of marriage. They chose to go ahead with their plans, so I had to accept that and keep my concerns to myself. It was difficult but important for our relationship.
>
> Shortly after they married, my husband offered them a copy of a personal finance program we have found helpful. He was

careful to tell them we were not implying they could not manage, we were simply sharing a program we have found helpful for our own marriage, and they could do whatever they wanted with it. They are using some of those basic principles and living a very happy life right now; and we are learning how to offer information without telling them what they need to do.

> We need to ask God to grant us wisdom and grace to know how to respond to the choices of our children and their mates, those we applaud and those that concern us.

Ultimately, we need to ask God to grant us wisdom and grace to know how to respond to the choices of our children and their mates, those we applaud and those that concern us, and to help us keep our concerns from becoming roadblocks to building a healthy relationship with them.

When Our Married Children Struggle

Amy and I have talked often during our coaching sessions about the challenges of parenting when a child and his spouse have disagreements and one or both of them come to you. She has watched her married children struggle at various times, and one even go through a divorce. She shares with us here how she handles these situations:

> If there's a healthy marriage, it's easier to talk to them when there's a disagreement. I find I can talk to the person who came to me, but first I must listen, listen, listen. Then I ask them what they could have done better, not what the other spouse should have done. I try to give both sides honor and merit. Then I try to work on the tools that can help make the one who came to me better able to deal with the real issues, not just the one that was discussed between them. When the marriage is unhealthy,

it's a very difficult balancing act for me as a parent and as a mother-in-law. The door is not always open for my counsel and the truth is not always welcomed. I struggle to know if voicing my concerns helps bring understanding or fuels their contention. And I don't want them to close the door on our relationship if they don't like what I say.

When our children are struggling with their spouses, our need to remain objective and respect boundaries can be at odds with our desire to protect our children. It's difficult to keep from defending them if they're criticized, or disciplining them if we know they are responsible for the conflict. We must also keep in mind that our children or their spouses may come to us simply to vent to someone they believe will understand—someone who cares. And we must remember that ultimately, they must work out their marriage issues themselves. Our role is to support them with our love and prayers, along with encouragement to work together to reconcile their differences.

If you become concerned about possible harm, such as abuse or illegal activities, talk to your child and urge him/her to seek safety and professional help. Be ready to help them find assistance if they ask you to do so. You may want to seek professional counsel to determine how to express your concerns safely and effectively, and to identify resources for your child.

Amy shares how she copes with the challenge of responding to her children's marital struggles:

> You want to protect your child. That desire never ends. But when an adult child has a conflict with a spouse, you must step away from direct involvement and pray, then pray some more. Taking sides or criticizing does not help—you or them. In fact, it usually only adds wood to the fire.
>
> As much as I know that's true, there have been times when I struggled to keep my protectiveness in check. I knew that I should,

but as a parent who loves and cares for my child above all else, I sometimes let my feelings for my child override my feelings about their marriage, which complicated things for all of us. It's hard to step back, but it is so important to learn how and when to share your thoughts and when to keep quiet.

I've learned I need to step away and weep for them, pray for them, and hurt with them but not try to fix it for them. Not an easy thing for me to do. I try to give advice only when asked and have even suggested on occasion that they seek outside counseling to understand the situation more objectively and learn how to work through conflicts. Ultimately, I've been learning to turn the whole thing over to God and trust Him. It's not easy, but it is so important, for me and for my sons and their spouses.

In-Law, Not Out-Law

I remember when my husband and I became "mother-in-law" and "father-in-law." Friends shared stories about great relationships between in-laws, yet we also heard sighs and cautions about conflicts and tensions that unfortunately stir in some family relationships. It's a challenging role, and the relationship is based on the contributions of both parents and adult children.

Our role as parents is to offer our best to our family relationships. It takes time, self-control, patience, sensitivity, effort, and determination to help foster positive and growing relationships with our children and their spouses. But the rewards for us and for our families are certainly worth the effort. Whether you are just now beginning this new role as an in-law or have been one for some time, there are steps you can take to help foster the best relationship possible with your child, his spouse, and your child's in-laws.

Get to know your son- or daughter-in-law, their interests, hobbies, talents, and work. Know their favorite foods and beverages, their birthdays, or other special events in their lives. Consider activities or projects you can plan together—things you would both enjoy.

For example, my daughter-in-law and I recently worked on a home decorating project together. Maybe you enjoy sports, shopping, cooking, or working in the garden. As you spend time together, quietly observe their frustrations and challenges. Pray privately about any concerns, but don't offer advice unless asked.

When your child and spouse visit, do all you can to make your home welcoming and comfortable for them, from favorite foods to a comfortable guest room, and a schedule that takes their desires into account. When you visit their home, offer to help, but don't get in the way. Do what you can to make the visit comfortable for all. In both situations, respect their privacy.

If your child and his spouse are living with you, set and communicate clear expectations about how you will function together. Work as a team to create a plan that will be comfortable for all of you. A friend's daughter and son-in-law lived with her for a time after the young couple's home sustained major storm damage. They worked out a rotation schedule for grocery shopping, cooking, cleaning, yard work, and even entertaining.

As your child is developing this new partnership, it's important to honor that relationship and never criticize one in front of the other. Be careful to avoid giving unsolicited advice or meddling in their issues. As you adjust to this new family dynamic, be sensitive to everyone's needs and focus on the overall goal of supporting them and nurturing your relationship. It's also helpful to foster a spirit of grace, a willingness to be flexible, and a sense of humor.

As you build a relationship with your new son- or daughter-in-law, encourage a respectful, cordial relationship with his/her parents. Ask your child to share information with you about their background that would be helpful for you to know. Look for opportunities to share family experiences and offer to coordinate schedules so that your child and spouse can spend time with both families, especially during holidays.

It's a blessing when friendships form between the parents of married adult children and they enjoy sharing special events and everyday life experiences. This is especially helpful when grandchildren come along. However, some families don't blend as easily and the connection between in-laws remains distant, even competitive. Parents need to be careful if this strain is present so it doesn't cause conflicts or divisiveness between the young married couple. Hannah was excited about the prospects of expanding family ties:

> When our son got married, we thought we would be one big happy family and would socialize with our future daughter-in-law's parents, especially since we live in the same city. We had the official meeting of the parents that was cordial but brief. Then we tried to get together with them again both before and after the wedding, and we came to the realization that they were not interested in developing a close relationship with us. We get along so well with our daughter's in-laws, so it feels awkward to have a strain with our son's in-laws. We love our new daughter-in-law, and that is the relationship we need to focus on. Her parents are her parents, but we are not going to become close to them. I hope things will soften some with time for the benefit of our children and grandchildren that may come along.

If You Sense a Strain With an In-Law . . .

Recognize that relationships are based on the contributions—the give and take—from each person. Sometimes one does not want to build a positive relationship with the other. If that's your situation and your son- or daughter-in-law doesn't want to establish a close relationship with you, don't try to force it to happen. The same is true with your child's in-laws.

If you are concerned, first take an honest look to see if you have done/are doing anything that would contribute to the conflicts. If the door is open, try communicating, using some of the communication tools for coaching and for mending fences mentioned earlier in this book. You may also want to seek counseling support to help you understand relationship dynamics and how you can best respond to the situation. Sometimes there are underlying issues that you cannot resolve, issues that may not even pertain to you directly. You may need to shift your expectations for the relationship and accept it as it is, as you seek God's guidance and grace.

> Look for open doors of opportunity to offer your love, respect, encouragement, patience, understanding, forgiveness, and prayer as the couple builds what you hope will be a positive, growing relationship.

Let your goal be to do your best to foster a healthy relationship with your child, his spouse, and your child's in-laws. Look for open doors of opportunity to offer your love, respect, encouragement, patience, understanding, forgiveness, and prayer as the couple builds what you hope will be a positive, growing relationship.

Becoming a Grandparent

For years I heard friends talk about how great it is to be a grandparent. They talked about a special depth of love, a fresh experience of joy, and a renewed energy that comes with the role. Each time I heard their stories, I would smile and respond, "That's nice, I'm glad for you." And I was; I just couldn't relate. That is, until it was my turn to receive that most precious gift: a grandchild. Oh, my goodness!

Now I know, firsthand, what my friends have been telling me. What a blessing has come into the life of our family through the birth of this little girl. It has taken me to a unique place of joy and wonder as I watch my son and daughter-in-law step into the role of parents and as I look into the eyes of that darling little one. I laugh and cry. I dream and plan. I pray for protection and care for her. And I ask God to grant me wisdom and grace to be the grandmother she needs me to be. I've also been told a sense of humor is important, as my friend Jeanette cautions:

> As for funny stories, that's one of the best parts of being grandparents. We have many to share because grandchildren are brutally honest in their observations and have a lovely way of putting you in your place. For instance, a few months ago my four-year-old granddaughter was sitting on the back of the sofa while I was holding her new baby brother. I thought she was studying his little face, but no—she was studying mine. Suddenly, she asked me, "Will your wrinkles disappear when you go to Heaven?" I had to think long and hard about her Christmas gifts! Grandchildren are truly God's gift to help us through the trials of aging.

While grandparenting can have humorous and playful moments, it's also a very challenging time. Some grandparents live close by and have an open door to share many special times with their grandchildren. Others live far away and seldom see theirs. Sadly, some grandparents have a strained relationship with their children and, consequently, may not see their grandchildren at all. Then there are grandparents who have the full-time responsibility for raising their grandchildren. Whatever your situation, it is important to build the best relationship you can with your grandchildren—and with their parents.

Grandparenting Tips

One of my favorite grandparenting quotes is credited to Rudolph Giuliani: "What children need most are the essentials that grandparents provide in abundance. They give unconditional love, kindness, patience, humor, comfort, lessons in life, and most importantly, cookies."

While I don't claim to have the best cookie recipes in town, I do know God has taught me powerful lessons about life, about himself, and about relationships. Now that I'm a grandparent, I must ask Him to help me pass along what I've learned. What lessons have you learned and how can you draw on them as you share life with your grandchildren? Several friends have shared their grandparenting tips with me, now that I've joined them in this role. Here are suggestions from their experiences that may be helpful for you to consider.

Plan events with your grandchildren that will be enjoyable, creative memory-makers. Include special occasions and also informal, playful times. Share traditions and perhaps begin new ones. One of my friends spends the day after Thanksgiving each year with her grandchildren, baking Christmas cookies to share with friends over the holidays. Another spends time with each grandchild at the end of the school year to celebrate their previous year's accomplishments and "graduation" to a new grade.

Learn about your grandchildren's interests and abilities so you can choose activities and gifts that are appropriate for them. Know about the sports they play or what groups they are part of and attend their special events when you can. Encourage learning and share time together with books, music, and the arts. Keep in mind that their interests and abilities change quickly. Share your own hobbies and things you enjoy with them as they are able to participate.

Treat each of your grandchildren as special and unique, respecting their talents and abilities as well as their challenges. Spend time with them individually as you can and perhaps plan special events for them, either one-on-one or in small groups. One of my friends has a "cousins' camp" each summer for her grandchildren to spend time together at Nana's house. The girls have tea parties, sewing lessons, and all sorts of fun activities to share—special memories to treasure.

Don't let your desire to spoil your grandchildren get out of hand or cause problems for their parents. Respect your children's rules and ask them how they want you to discipline their children so you can be consistent when they are in your care. Don't allow your grandchildren to disrespect you or say disrespectful things about their parents when you are caring for them. In turn, don't criticize your children in front of your grandchildren. Don't interfere when your children are disciplining their children and don't challenge their authority or their rules. If you have a concern, talk with your children privately to work it through in a way that is comfortable for all.

Grandchild-proof your home before your grandchildren come to visit. Carefully examine each room to see what your little ones will see and reach out for. When I taught school many years ago, I remember my kindergarten teacher friends telling me that after they set up their classroom each year, they would go through the room on their knees so they could see things from their young students' view. As a new grandmother, I think it's a great idea for us to apply as we prepare for our grandchildren to visit. Look for things that can be tugged on, slipped on, toppled over, opened up, ingested, tampered with, or torn apart. Watch for sharp corners, poisonous plants, glass that can easily break, doors that can be locked/unlocked, and other potential dangers. Check the outside areas of your home also and remember that older children are curious as well. Are fire extinguishers, emergency kits, and phone numbers up-to-date? Do you have the information you would need in the event of an emergency while the grandchildren are in your care?

Take the initiative to talk to your grandchildren on the telephone or through Internet connections. Ask about what is going on in their lives. Then listen when they share; don't rush them through the conversation. Send them a letter, an e-mail note, or a card—not just on birthdays or holidays, but at unexpected times as well. Let them know you are thinking of them. Contact them before their special events to wish them well.

Take advantage of every opportunity you can to affirm your grandchildren and let them know they are valuable, first and foremost as God's children, and also because they have much to offer your family, their friends, and the world in which they live. Tell them, "I believe in you and I'm proud of you." Let them know, "God loves you very much and so do I." Compliment them when they exhibit positive character traits such as kindness, helpfulness, patience, honesty, or consideration of others. Praise them when you know they have tried their best to accomplish something, regardless of the outcome. Positive affirmation builds their self-confidence that in turn encourages them to give their best effort in whatever they are doing.

> Be available to them emotionally and physically as you can, while also balancing your own needs and schedule.

Respect the role of other grandparents in the lives of your grandchildren and avoid words or actions that would appear competitive, critical, or would interfere with those other relationships. Offer understanding, compromise, and flexibility as you share time and special occasions with the other grandparents.

A Few More Grandparenting Tips

Let your grandchildren know you are praying for them. If you know they are facing a challenging time like the first day of school, a test, a performance, a ball game, an important decision to make, a relationship problem, or perhaps a struggle of some kind, let them know you will pray for them during that time. That encouragement empowers them and gives you an opportunity to show your love in action.

Be the kind of grandparent your children and grandchildren can depend upon. Keep your word. Show them, as well as tell them, that you love and support them. Respect them, as you ask them to respect you. Be available to them emotionally and physically as you can, while also balancing your own needs and schedule. Remember, as you take care of yourself, you are modeling the behavior you encourage in them.

Changes come and problems arise, sometimes for the grand-children and sometimes for their parents. Unexpected needs come along and grandparents need to be able to adapt when necessary. Recognize that your children are learning how to be parents and developing their own parenting styles that may have some similar-ity to yours and some aspects that are very different. Be flexible, respectful, patient, supportive, and complimentary whenever you can. Ask God to guide them and to help you to be the right kind of support as they raise their children.

If Your Child's Marriage Ends

One of the most difficult challenges parents face is watching their children suffer. When it comes to their relationships, we are hopeful that their friendships and marriages will last a lifetime. However, we know that sometimes marriages end through death or divorce. Whether or not we believe the ending is warranted, we still grieve for them and with them. We don't want them to struggle and yet we know they must ultimately travel that recovery journey on their own.

Our role is to be present with our love and prayers, and to pro-vide support when they ask. Their decisions are ultimately theirs to make and to work through, and we must be careful not to compound their grief and adjustments with our comments and criticisms of them and of their spouses.

If you find yourself in this position, recognize that you have your own grief to work through as you let go of dreams and expectations you had for your child, and as you let go of the person your child brought into your life. Find safe, healthy ways to process your feelings and confidential, caring people to help you deal with your own concerns so your grief does not complicate your child's situation.

If you have grandchildren, be careful to manage your emotions so that you can be in a healthy position to offer them your support, attention, stability, and assurance that you are there for them. Watch how you answer their questions and don't criticize their parents. Express your concerns if they ask, but don't elaborate on your own feelings. Encourage them to talk with their parents about their questions and feelings. If your children remarry, do all you can to help your grandchildren adjust to their new blended family. Support your child and grandchildren by welcoming new spouses and new stepgrandchildren that may come along.

Caring for Your Family Tree

If nurtured and lovingly cared for, the relationships between parents and their children—and between grandparents and their grandchildren—will carry on through life's greatest joys, deepest sorrows, and most difficult challenges. Ask the Lord to strengthen, protect, and deepen those relationships and to fill your heart with His love to share with your family—love that will last a lifetime.

On a Personal Note

Are your children married or planning to marry? If so, how are you showing your support for their choices and how are you managing your concerns? What steps will you take to strengthen the relationship between you and your child, and between you and his partner?

Have you stepped into the role of grandparent? If so, consider the tips mentioned and choose a few that you will focus on as you seek ways to offer your love and support to your grandchildren and to their parents as well.

Chapter Seven

Bring Your Children Before the Lord

"When I'm praying, I see it more like a lifetime assignment from God to keep my adult children covered, so that His will can be done in their lives."
—STORMIE OMARTIAN, *THE POWER OF PRAYING FOR YOUR ADULT CHILDREN*

Our adult children face numerous challenges as they embrace this new life passage, and we want to support them in every way possible. We can offer wise counsel and help when asked. We can step aside and encourage them to take responsibility for their lives as we establish healthy roles and boundaries. We can offer praise and excitement in their victories and comfort in their losses. Yet the most powerful gift of love we can give is to lift our children up in prayer to God, who ultimately has their lives in His hands. It is our greatest privilege and our utmost responsibility as parents.

I remember praying for my children during those first few days of their lives as I looked ahead with hopes and dreams for them. I prayed when they started school as I considered the people who would influence them—both teachers and friends. My prayers for them stepped up considerably when they began driving and as they dealt with the challenges of being a teenager. Then they stepped into the role of adult as they went away to college and began building their own lives. I now realize how little control I have over their choices and futures. I know that the opportunities, challenges, and decisions are greater than ever before, and the only way they can successfully manage them will be with God's help. So I continue to pray for them.

My children need God's wisdom to make the right choices for their lives. They need His protection from temptations that would distract them from the path God has planned for them. They need a keen awareness of His presence and the comfort of His promises as they face success and failure, joy and sorrow.

Now that my sons are adults, I realize more than ever before the need to pray for them (and for my daughter-in-law and grand-daughter as well). They need the support I can offer as I bring my petitions for them to the Lord. And I need the comfort of knowing that while they are in control of their own lives, I still have a vital part to play by praying for them. When I talk to God about my children, I feel a sense of partnership with Him. I share my heart and ask Him to intervene, and He reminds me of His love for them and His desire to work in their lives. As I listen to Him, I grow in my understanding of Him and deepen my faith in His love, His mercy, His grace, and His power.

Perhaps you've been praying for your children daily since they were born. Or maybe you began after a key event in their lives. You may be at a place now where you recognize the power and potential that is available to you and your children and you want to begin praying for them. As parents of adult children, the opportunity is ours to show our love for them by talking to God about them and listening as He shares His heart with us. So let's consider how to pray in a way that honors God, supports our children, and strengthens our own spiritual life.

It's About Them . . . *and* It's About Us

It's important for us to believe that while we cannot change our adult children's lives directly, God can change everything, as long as someone's heart is open to Him. In order for us to pray for them confidently, we must believe that God loves them and that His power to hear and answer our prayers is greater than any problems they may experience. Since we so rarely know what is happening in their hearts, we need to pray and trust God to work, believing He knows what is best for our children and is at work in their lives, even when we don't understand what's happening. With those beliefs we'll find the hope that will guide our thoughts and guard our hearts as we carry our concerns for our children to the Lord.

As we come to know God more intimately ourselves, we can have an open, honest, from-the-heart dialogue with Him as we share our concerns, our fears, and our desires. Sometimes we know just what to pray as we become aware of what is happening in our children's lives. Perhaps they've come to us with their problems, asked for our help, or asked us to pray for them about something.

There are other times when we sense something is not quite right, but our children are quiet about whatever may be happening. We find ourselves concerned, yet unsure about just how to pray. How comforting it is to know that God knows exactly what is going on. Sometimes He gives me an impression or insight and I know just how to pray, while at other times He simply draws me close to Him and whispers in my ear, "Yes, there's a problem. You don't need to know the details, you just need to be still and trust me." I don't have to understand what is happening. I just have to bring my children before the Lord and focus on His love for them and His promises to them. When I do so, His peace overcomes my fear.

Then there are those times of crisis when I fall to my knees in fear, in pain, in disappointment, feeling helpless as I cry out for God to intervene in the life of my child. It's the only thing I know to do in those times, yet it is the very thing I need to do. Bringing my child before God and placing my trust in Him is the best way I can love my child and support him in that moment.

I'd like to tell you that when those times have come, I have simply released my sense of control and stood confidently on the sidelines, watching and waiting for God to bring about change in my child's life. But I must admit, the act of letting go is the hardest thing I've been called to do, especially when I fear the outcome might not be what I think best. If I'm not careful, my worries can get the best of me physically and emotionally, weighing me down, interfering with other relationships, distracting me from the things I need to do, and robbing me of joy. Yet when I do release my child into God's hands, His peace overcomes my fear as He reminds me of His power, His promises, and His love for my children.

> It's a continual growth journey of asking, releasing, trusting, and expecting.

He also reminds me that whatever happens in the life of my children is between God and them. When I keep my focus there, I can release negativity and take on hope. I can pray with confidence and deepen my trust. And I begin to adopt an attitude of expectancy as I remind myself that God is in control. For me, it's a continual growth journey of asking, releasing, trusting, and expecting. Perhaps it is for you as well. How comforting to know God is faithful to accomplish what He wants to do in the lives of our children.

Rachel's Story

Rachel, like so many parents, knows the importance of praying for her children, especially now that they have stepped into adulthood and are tackling some of life's most difficult challenges. She shares a part of that prayer journey here:

> I find myself praying more now than I did in the past when my children were young. When they are little, you have more control over their environment and their friends and you are more of an influence in their lives. I find myself praying more as they have become adults and I don't have the control over their lives I once had.
>
> The first stage of letting go—or loosening control—happened when they started to drive. I couldn't go to sleep until they were home, praying they would survive the night. There were a whole new group of friends once they became mobile and I realized those friends had more influence than I did.
>
> Then they went away to college and I didn't know what they were doing. In some ways that was a comfort, but at other times my fear took over as I realized there was little I could do except pray and hope they would be okay. As adults, they are now making their own choices about careers, spouses, finances, and their lifestyle. While I can give my opinions, I can't control how they choose to live their lives.
>
> Recently, I experienced a situation that shook me like none other. My daughter had an anxiety attack and tried cutting herself, but went too deep and had sixteen stitches in her arm. The phone call from the hospital at three a.m. was the worst experience of my life. I was overwhelmed with fear as I drove the three hours to bring her home.
>
> While in high school, my daughter had done some cutting as a way of controlling her anxiety. With counseling, I thought we were past that, but then I received the phone call that turned me upside down. My daughter was drunk and was anxious about a visit from the family the next day, so while she was trying to clean up her apartment, she decided to cut herself to control the anxiety.
>
> I have never prayed as much in my life as I did that night and through the following two months. The hardest thing for a parent to do is to put a child's life in the hands of the Lord and

trust that He will do what is best. I held on to the belief that while I was powerless to heal her, God could. So I have been asking Him to heal her body, mind, and spirit, and to calm my fears as I learn to trust Him more. She has been in counseling and on antidepressants the past few months as she learns to deal with life and her parents, now that she is an adult. I am encouraged but I know I need to continue to pray for her each day. I'm praying for her counselor as well, asking God to guide that relationship with His wisdom and healing. It's perhaps the best way I can demonstrate my love for her and my trust in God's love for her. I don't know what the future holds, but I do know God holds our future in His hands and He'll guide us each step of the way.

Praying Specifically for Our Children

In her book *The Power of Praying for Your Adult Children*, author Stormie Omartian gives specific ways we can pray for our children. Her chapter titles suggest that as we bring our children before the Lord, we can pray that they will:

- See God Pour Out His Spirit Upon Them

- Develop a Heart for God, His Word, and His Ways

- Grow in Wisdom, Discernment, and Revelation

- Find Freedom, Restoration, and Wholeness

- Understand God's Purpose for Their Lives

- Work Successfully and Have Financial Stability

- Have a Sound Mind and a Right Attitude

- Resist Evil Influences and Destructive Behavior

- Avoid All Sexual Pollution and Temptation

- Experience Good Health and God's Healing

- Enjoy a Successful Marriage and Raise Godly Children

- Maintain Strong and Fulfilling Relationships

- Be Protected and Survive Tough Times

- Walk Into the Future God Has for Them[1]

As you consider these desires for your children's lives, ask God to show you areas where they may be struggling so you can pray more specifically for them. The more open and honest you are in your conversation with God, the more you will be able to release your concerns, fears, and desires into His hands. As you envision how His power, grace, mercy, and love can work in those areas of your children's lives, you'll find a stronger sense of hope and trust that He will answer your petition and work on their behalf according to His will.

Also consider aspects of your children's lives where you see growth and maturity, healing, positive steps, healthy choices, victories won, and God's blessing. Our prayer conversations with God are also times to celebrate what is going well, which fuels our hope as we call on Him with our concerns.

> Our prayer conversations with God are also times to celebrate what is going well, which fuels our hope as we call on Him with our concerns.

The Waiting Room

We can have a strong influence in the lives of our children, even if they seem to drift away from the path we believe God has for them or if they walk away from that path in rebellion. As we ask God to speak to their hearts, to protect them, and to intervene in their lives, He will create opportunities for them to turn toward Him, to hear Him, to sense His direction, and to follow His guidance. I've watched God open and close doors in the lives of my children often, prompting them to move in the direction He desires, and reminding me He is actively working in their lives.

As we offer our prayers and hold on to our faith, our children will also know we are lifting them up and will see a spirit of hope in us rather than a spirit of fear or discouragement. Many people's lives have turned around as the result of the faithful prayer of someone who was willing to stand in the gap for them and not give up.

My friend Nicole raised her children in a strong Christian environment. Each one had a personal relationship with God and had been involved in church activities growing up. But she became concerned when one of her sons began to drift away from his faith as he became an adult and stepped out on his own. She talked to him often about her concerns but felt her words were falling on deaf ears. She knew at that point the only thing she could do was to ask God to speak to his heart in ways she couldn't, and to draw her son back to Him through the influence of others in his life.

> When I knew my adult child would not listen to me anymore, I began to pray for a Christian spouse for him. Even though I knew my son was not living a good Christian life, I knew that a Christian spouse would influence him and impact the makeup of a family he might someday have. God answered my prayers by bringing a wonderful girl into his life—one that we already knew. Now I am happy to say that my son has married a Christian young woman and as a result of her influence has a closer walk with God. Also, he now has a daughter that has brought him even closer to God, and he realizes the importance of raising his child in the church.

As we pray for our children, we often have the opportunity to see God's hand at work, and it's exciting when an answer comes as it did for Nicole in the life of her son. And yet it doesn't always happen just that way, does it? There are times when we pray and see answers almost as soon as we've finished the prayer. Other times, however, we find ourselves in the waiting room, wondering when God will answer us. Wondering when change will come in the lives of our children. Sometimes fighting doubts and fears, always clinging to the hope that God did hear and will answer—in His way, in His time. We find ourselves asking, "How long do we wait? How long does it take for God to get their attention? How long before they will come back to what we believe is the right path for their lives?"

I wish I could say that our children always turn their lives around and restoration always takes place. But when I look into the eyes of many parents, and as I consider my own journey as a parent, I realize that healing and renewal don't always happen when and how we wish they would. It's during those times when we must hold on to our understanding of God's power, His promises, and His provision. Hold on to our belief in His love for our children, trusting that He does hear us and will answer according to His will and in His timing.

> No matter what the outcome, I know God is in control. In that belief, I can find a peace that surpasses my understanding, love that will guard my heart, and wisdom that will guide my steps.

We must also hold on to the truth that our children are God's children and ultimately, whatever happens in their lives is between God and them. We must let go of our desire to control the situation and release responsibility for the outcome so we can hold on to the truths that will guide us.

When I'm in life's waiting room, looking for answers to prayers, I find one of the most encouraging steps I can take is to reflect on God's love, power, mercy, and grace. I focus on the ways He has made himself known to me and how I have seen Him work in my life and in the lives of those I love. I reflect on how He has blessed the one I am praying specifically for and how He has blessed me. Then I can begin to pray words of thanksgiving and words of expectancy as I look forward to how God will again demonstrate His love. No matter what the outcome, I know God is in control. In that belief, I can find a peace that surpasses my understanding, love that will guard my heart, and wisdom that will guide my steps.

A Time to Speak and a Time to Listen

In her book *A Long Way Off*, author Kitti Murray speaks of prayer as "a holy calling, a deep dialogue, a relationship, a bond between those who pray and the King of heaven, who starts the conversation to begin with."[2]

Prayer is not intended to be a ritual we practice out of habit or a means of winning God's love or approval. It's an intimate conversation between a loving Father and His child. Kitti reminds us that God began the conversation, and when we talk to Him about our children, we have the opportunity to hear Him remind us of what He has already spoken to us in His Word.

Our conversation with Him is more than just a list of our concerns and His response of what He will or will not do. It is a heart-to-heart connection that flows in both directions as He invites us into His presence and we share time with Him. We have the opportunity to express our love and reflect on the amazing love He has for us—His children. He has already begun speaking and is waiting for us to join Him. I've heard it said that prayer involves exhaling our doubts and fears and inhaling God's Spirit. As we exhale our praises and our petitions, we can inhale His love and promises. Our focus shifts from lamenting our problems to anticipating His solutions.

Let these verses from God's Word serve as a guide for your

thoughts and encouragement for your spirit as you talk with Him about your adult children and as you listen for His voice to speak to your heart.

Do not be anxious about anything, but in every situation, by prayer and petition, with thanksgiving, present your requests to God. And the peace of God, which transcends all understanding, will guard your hearts and your minds in Christ Jesus. Finally, brothers and sisters, whatever is true, whatever is noble, whatever is right, whatever is pure, whatever is lovely, whatever is admirable—if anything is excellent or praiseworthy—think about such things. Whatever you have learned or received or heard from me, or seen in me—put it into practice. And the God of peace will be with you.

—PHILIPPIANS 4:6–9

And we know that in all things God works for the good of those who love him, who have been called according to his purpose.

—ROMANS 8:28

I sought the Lord, and he answered me; he delivered me from all my fears.

—PSALM 34:4

Many are the woes of the wicked but the Lord's unfailing love surrounds the man who trusts in him.

—PSALM 32:10

Jesus replied, "What is impossible with man is possible with God."

—LUKE 18:27

Ask and it will be given to you; seek and you will find; knock and the door will be opened to you. For everyone who asks receives; the one who seeks finds; and to the one who knocks, the door will be opened.

—MATTHEW 7:7–8

Devote yourselves to prayer, being watchful and thankful.

—COLOSSIANS 4:2

This is the confidence we have in approaching God: that if we ask anything according to his will, he hears us. And if we know that he hears us—whatever we ask—we know that we have what we asked of him.

—1 JOHN 5:14–15

For the eyes of the Lord range throughout the earth to strengthen those whose hearts are fully committed to him.

—2 CHRONICLES 16:9

"Because he loves me," says the Lord, "I will rescue him; I will protect him, for he acknowledges my name. He will call upon me, and I will answer him; I will be with him in trouble, I will deliver him and honor him. With long life will I satisfy him and show him my salvation."

—PSALM 91:14–16

The Lord is good to those whose hope is in him, to the one who seeks him; It is good to wait quietly for the salvation of the Lord. . . . For no one is cast off by the Lord forever. Though he brings grief, he will show compassion, so great is his unfailing love.

—LAMENTATIONS 3:25–26; 31–33

But blessed is the one who trusts in the Lord, whose confidence is in him. They will be like a tree planted by the water that sends out its roots by the stream. It does not fear when heat comes; its leaves are always green. It has no worries in a year of drought and never fails to bear fruit.

—JEREMIAH 17:7–8

"What no eye has seen, what no ear has heard, and what no human mind has conceived"—the things God has prepared for those who love him—these are the things God has revealed to us by his Spirit.

—1 CORINTHIANS 2:9–10

On a Personal Note

How would you like to incorporate the gift of praying for your children into your daily life? What steps will you take to create a quiet, uninterrupted time and place to talk with your heavenly Father about the children you both love?

Consider the opportunities and challenges your children are currently facing. You may want to begin a prayer journal as you write down your concerns and as you record how you see God at work in their lives and what He is teaching you.

Choose some passages from God's Word, like those mentioned in this chapter, to guide you as you talk with God about your children. As you pray, allow time to pour out your heart. Allow time to be still as you listen for His voice. And allow time to praise Him for who He is and all that He has promised for you and for your children.

145

Chapter Eight

Manage Special Challenges With Education and Support

"I am only one, but I am one. I cannot do everything, but I can do something. And I will not let what I cannot do interfere with what I can do."
—EDWARD EVERETT HALE, AUTHOR

As we anxiously awaited the birth of our children, we dreamed about how life would be for them—a childhood full of wonder and joy. We believed we would share exciting experiences with them as they grew into happy, healthy, well-adjusted adults. Oh, we knew we'd face difficulties along the way, but we firmly believed all would be okay and life would be just as we planned for both our children and ourselves. Then we carefully tucked our dreams and wishes into a nice, neat little box called the future, which we tied with a ribbon of hope. We set our box on the shelf of expectation and began our parenting journey, confident all would go according to plan.

Perhaps some of it did. But we know that life has a way of taking unexpected twists and turns. Our lives—and those of our children—don't always fit into our nice, neat little box of wishes and dreams. Whether we anticipate it or not, whether we are ready or not, challenges come into the lives of those we love, bringing along changes and choices for us to address with them. Some of those challenges are exciting, whether planned or unexpected. They cause us to shift our plans as we joyfully support our children and watch the future unfold. Other struggles come along in their lives either suddenly or over time that seem to tear our hearts apart with disappointment and sometimes pain. We must set aside our plans and expectations as we come to terms with the changes taking place in their lives and in our own as we determine how best to support them.

A child who becomes a single parent. One who struggles with an addiction. A child born with a disability or one who suffers with a chronic or acute illness or injury. One who struggles with a mental health disorder. A child who travels abroad to serve in the military, or one who must serve time in prison.

> Our attitude will play a vital role in how we respond to the challenges that come and how we help our children deal with them.

When our children face special challenges like these, we must do all we can to love and support them in healthy, constructive ways that are best for both us and them. It may mean we have to unpack the box of dreams and plans we formed in our minds and hearts when they were young. We can take out whatever dreams no longer fit, add new hopes and plans, bind it together with new expectations, and set it on a shelf supported with the promises of God's love and provision.

If we want to support our children through life's challenges, we must educate ourselves, recognize the impact of their struggles on both their lives and our own, and take steps to care for ourselves as we care for them. We may need to alter current boundaries and set more reasonable ones as we shift our expectations. It will be important for us to surround ourselves with support and ask God to equip us with the tools we need to successfully embrace whatever life brings. And we'll need to support our children as they take those same steps.

Our attitude will play a vital role in how we respond to the challenges that come and how we help our children deal with them. While we may not have any control over the situation, we do have control over the attitude we choose to embrace. We can ask God to help us find meaning and purpose in our lives as we learn to adapt and move forward with a positive spirit. And we can look for ways to exercise our humor muscles. There is power, release, connection with others, and healing in laughter as it eases tension and helps us move through life's difficulties. The challenge itself may not be humorous, but we can carefully and respectfully look for ways to lighten our heavy hearts and bring a smile or two.

While the details of the traumas or challenges our children face differ, we may experience similar struggles and find common strategies we can incorporate as we work to address our needs and theirs. I've included stories about two areas of challenge that many parents face, to give examples of insight and guidance in how to effectively respond. At the close of the chapter, you'll also find a list of resources that offer education and support for various life challenges—some of which you may be facing yourself.

A Military Wife Shares Her Thoughts

Sara Horn is the wife of a Navy Reservist, the founder of Wives of Faith (*www.wivesoffaith.org*), and the author of *GOD Strong: A Military Wife's Spiritual Survival Guide*. I talked with her recently about the challenges unique to families of those in the military and asked her to comment about the varying perspectives of parents and spouses of those serving.

There has always been an interesting dynamic between the mother of a soldier and the wife of a soldier. Since I interact mainly with the wives of soldiers, I have heard countless stories of the "crazy" mother-in-law—the one who seems to cry more than the spouse at the mere mention of a deployment. Or the one who insists on the soldier coming home to her house for R&R instead of to his wife and their home. Or the one who doesn't connect or stay in touch at all with the spouse or even the service member while he serves overseas.

Parents and spouses have different perspectives when it comes to their loved one serving in uniform. Both love, but the parent also wants to protect; the spouse wants to support. These are two vastly different viewpoints, which in turn can offer very different emotions.

Sara travels throughout the country, spending time with many wives whose husbands are serving in the military. I asked if she would pass along some advice to parents who want to be the best support to their children in the military and to the spouses and families of those serving. Her comments are directed toward parents who have a son serving, but she shares the same advice with those who have a daughter in the military.

First recognize the important service your son is performing for his country and be proud of him. Whether or not you agree with his decision to join the military (especially if you don't agree with the current wars), your child has made a decision to serve the greater good and do something that makes a difference for others. Surely you can be proud of that.

When it comes to supporting the spouse of your soldier, be sensitive to her needs as well as her emotions. Deployment is an incredibly emotional thing and it can be hard to gauge sometimes what everyone wants or needs. Don't be afraid to ask your daughter-in-law what she needs from you. Is it help with the grandkids? A listening ear? Prayer?

Don't go to your soldier son's wife and complain about his

military service, or express your serious fears about his being overseas. You need another friend to talk to about these issues. Your daughter-in-law has enough fear and stress of her own, and it is a difficult role to live as the wife versus the mom. For the wife, it isn't just about the heartstrings—she is living it on a daily basis as she keeps her home going, her kids going, and encourages her husband while he's away.

I realize I'm listing a lot of don'ts here—how about some do's?

Do offer your daughter-in-law and grandchildren your full support and let them know you're available to help as they need it. Give specifics of how you can help. For example, if you live close enough, volunteer to have a Grammy night once a week so your daughter-in-law can have a little break. Or make plans to visit as often as you're able and show your support in tangible ways.

Do give your daughter-in-law the right-of-way when it comes to any decisions regarding the deployment—departure, R&R, homecoming. Honor Ephesians 5:31, and recognize your son is now the head of his own household. You don't have to remove yourself completely from the equation. Let them know if you'd like to be part of the departure or homecoming festivities, but be sensitive to what they may be feeling. Don't demand—request. Respect your adult child and his spouse's wishes if they just want themselves and children to be together before/after he leaves or comes back.

Be a blessing to your grandchildren. Offer them encouragement and tell them often how proud you are of them and what they're accomplishing while their parent is gone.

Use this deployment to grow closer to your daughter-in-law and grandchildren.

More Military Family Tips

Sara spoke about the importance of being sensitive to the needs of each family member, so you will want to be mindful of that when your military son comes home. If you live in another town and want to spend time with the family, consider saving your visit for a week or two after your child arrives home. Ask when the couple will feel ready for you to visit and be prepared that it may be several weeks later. Consider meeting somewhere for a vacation and include time for them to be alone as well as time together with you. If you live away from your child's spouse and children, invite and pay for them to come visit you while your military child is away on active duty, if you can afford to do so. As you send cards and gifts to your child, also send cards and gifts and make calls to your child's spouse and children. Remind them that you care for them as well and you are supporting the entire family.

My friend Evelyn understands, firsthand, the challenges for a military mom. I asked her how she coped with the challenges she faced while her son was in training and then overseas.

The Marineparents.com Web site and the wonderful people we connected with through it were my lifeline from the time my son joined and left for boot camp until after he got home from Iraq. We shared our emotions, any news we received, and tips for coping with the stress we experienced. I would strongly recommend connecting with other parents in every way possible. The Lord also brought total strangers into my life at my weakest moments to give encouragement. Prayer first, Web site second!

I also wrote to my son every day. I took random pictures of everyday life and sent him something every day. I sent boxes of stuff every couple of weeks, and I also did a massive e-mail update to friends and family. It was like a newsletter that kept everyone informed and kept me sane because I felt like I was a vital part of my son's experience. We (moms) used to have contests to see who could pack the most weight and send the most to our children. It was practical, and it was also a fun way to encourage each other as we supported our children.

One word of caution I would give parents: When my son came home, I was full of pride in him and his service to our country, but I had to be careful not to put him on a "hero" pedestal that pressured him to be something he wasn't. I saw that happening as some young men and women struggled to find their places in civilian life when they returned home. My son needs my love, encouragement, patience, and prayers as he settles in and moves forward with his life—in his own way and in his own time.

When Children Face Illness and Disability

When we see our children struggle with a physical or mental health challenge, our heart aches as we realize we cannot fix it for them. We cannot simply kiss their "boo-boo" and "make it all better." Some pains last for a short time, others for a lifetime. They hurt, and we hurt with them as we stand on the sidelines with tear-filled eyes, wishing we could make the pain go away. Asking God to intervene. Praying for a miracle. Wondering how we will all adapt. Learning how to work through our grief so we can find a way to cope. Trying to support our child while not losing ourselves in the process. Looking for answers. Reaching out for support. Adjusting to what may become a "new normal" in our lives. Hoping that in the midst of pain, sorrow, and uncertainty, we'll somehow find peace and even joy.

If your child has struggled since he was young, perhaps even since birth, you've most likely learned how to adapt as you've cared for him. Now that he's grown, you need to understand how his struggles impact him as an adult so you can determine the best support to provide at this stage of his life—and yours. You may need to continue some means of care already in place while making adjustments in other areas as you look ahead to the future.

Some of you may have a child who more recently developed an illness or injury, perhaps even suddenly, and you must learn how to help him—and yourself—respond to the trauma and move forward. It may involve a temporary time of treatment and healing, or it may be the emergence of a chronic or ongoing challenge that will require more long-term treatment and care. You've suddenly found yourself, your child, even your family in an unexpected place in life as you realize your sense of normal may be shifting.

Whether you've just stepped into this support role or have been there for some time, there are steps you can take to better understand the scope of your child's illness or disability so you can determine how to best support him and take care of yourself as well. Begin by clarifying your role: a parent who will offer support in healthy ways as you partner with your child to help him live his best life. Maintain respect for your child as an adult, encourage him to care for himself as much as he can, and offer supplemental assistance as needed.

Research the illness/disability to understand the most current information regarding diagnosis, treatment options, and care. Consult with medical professionals who can offer both insight and advice for you and your child. Clarify his abilities and limitations. Are they temporary or permanent? What kind of care does he need to function at his best? Can he take care of himself independently in a healthy and safe manner or will he need assistance? What about the areas of transportation, living conditions, finances, medical care, and socialization? Are there certain boundaries you need to set regarding your involvement? Discuss information, options, and advice with your child, and encourage him to make decisions—to whatever extent he is able—whenever appropriate to do so.

It is vital that you take time to assess your own situation carefully as well as your child's. Then you can be clear about the extent and limitations of the support you can give and help your child plan with those boundaries in mind.

A word of caution: Before you have this discussion, consider your own emotions, needs, resources, and limitations as you determine the scope of support you can provide. Too often, parents jump in to help, declaring,

"I'll take care of whatever you need," only to realize later that they cannot meet all their child's needs and take care of their own needs in the process.

Even if parents can take care of their child adequately, they may be assuming more control than necessary, limiting their child's opportunity or necessity to care for himself as he can. Or they may be so overwhelmed by the challenges that they don't know what to do and don't think they can support their child effectively. So they pull back and rely on others to help their child. Yet there may in fact be steps they can personally take to support their child and foster a positive interaction that can strengthen their relationship.

If your child is dealing with a physical or mental illness or disability, it is vital that you take time to assess your own situation carefully as well as your child's. Then you can be clear about the extent and limitations of the support you can give and help your child plan with those boundaries in mind. You may want to locate resources and support to assist both you and your child as you determine how to successfully meet the challenges. An objective, informed person can help you assess your thoughts and plans to confirm that you and your child are working together as much as possible to make sound decisions and not let your emotions cloud your judgment.

One Mom's Story

Humor columnist Dixie Frantz writes about everyday life experiences, including stories about life with a daughter who has a disability. I asked her to share a few words, and here are her "confessions of a parent of an adult disabled child":

> My daughter, Melanie, was born with cerebral palsy. We don't know why. The reason has long ago ceased to be important.

That was over twenty-five years ago. She has never walked, can't read or write her name, and needs lots of care. Mentally, she is about four years old. That means she still loves her cartoons. We are talking *Dora the Explorer* and *SpongeBob SquarePants*. And yes, I will be the first to admit that purchasing Melanie the perfect birthday and Christmas presents sometimes makes me cry. It is so difficult to be age appropriate, which is what they tell you to be in school, when what Melanie really wants is the latest Talking Elmo. Her vocabulary is about 300 words, and she doesn't know the difference between today, tomorrow, and yesterday. Yep, all that might sound like a pretty sad life . . . for her . . . for me . . . and for the rest of the family. Personally, I allow myself a pity party for about ten seconds . . . once a year . . . and yes . . . she gets a new Elmo every year.

Melanie is also our angel, minus the actual wings, although I know for certain they are there . . . somewhere. She is extremely social and loving and gives the best hugs. She makes me smile from the minute I get her up in the morning till I put her to bed at night. Melanie has a wonderful life living at home with her parents, but it took a lot of work to get there. She goes to church every Sunday. We sit on the front row next to the choir and I hold her hand to keep her calm. Melanie's wheelchair fits perfect in that little spot. She hugs the priests, and many others, when it is time to go home. Melanie attends a local day center during the week, goes to camp in the summer for a week, attends a Fun Day program through the Arc of Greater Houston twice a month, and generally is well-known in the community in which we live.

It wasn't easy getting to this point in our collective lives. Did I mention that I have lots of friends with disabled adult children? We sought each other out and met once a month for years when our special children were young. We worked together first with our school district to make things better for our special-needs children. Then we reached out to our community, helping to create a program called Special Friends Night Out at our local YMCA. The YMCA provides the place and a few staff on a Saturday evening when the Y is officially closed. The cost is minimal. A couple of parents of those with special needs do a little training. School and church groups graciously provide teen volunteers.

Once a month for a few hours magic happens as those with special needs buddy with a teen volunteer to play basketball, sing karaoke, play games, dance, make crafts, play pool, and generally just hang out. Every YMCA in the country should have such a program. My disabled daughter has been attending since she was little and loves it. And Melanie's parents . . . they have a date night! It's a beautiful thing for our marriage and for our daughter.

I learned years ago that nobody is going to knock on your door and automatically sign your adult child up for anything. Someone in the family has to pick up the ball and run real fast with it. My biggest fear when Melanie graduated, or aged out of school, was that she would come home to spend the rest of her life staring at the television or me. I learned that if Melanie needed something, I would have to figure out a way to get it for her.

There is a mental health organization in our state that offers services to keep special children in their homes when they reach adult age. In Texas, MHMRA is the organization that has programs like respite and help with paying for attendance at a day center. But every state is different, making it a challenge to navigate without knowledge. Sometimes there are long waiting lists to receive certain services. Melanie has been on a list for assistance from our local Home and Community-Based Services Program that provides support and services to persons with disabilities living in their own home with family or a paid companion. We have been waiting for six years, and we figure we have another two years before her name comes up. I should have signed her up years ago. While your child is still in school, the school districts provide volumes of information to assist with making that scary transition to adulthood. Don't put the pile of information in a stack to collect dust. Read through the stuff, ask questions, and figure out if there is something in all those pages that will benefit your adult child. I believe if a program will improve the quality of Melanie's life it is totally worth the effort.

Tips for Parents

Dixie talks primarily about the needs of her adult daughter, but what about the needs of parents? For that, we can turn to professionals like Mary Yerkes, author, speaker, life coach, and founder of New Life Christian Coaching. She understands through both her personal and professional experience the impact that disability, extended illness, and other traumas can have on individuals and families.

> Parents of children in difficult situations experience vicarious trauma. Vicarious trauma, or compassion fatigue, is the stress reaction that occurs when you care about or for adult children who are mentally or physically ill, in dangerous situations, or facing trauma in their lives. It results in inner changes to your psychological, physical, and spiritual health and can put you at serious risk for depression, anxiety, addiction, and more. In situations like these it is common to feel powerless and robbed of options and choices, but that is not the case.

As a professional coach, Mary helps clients increase their awareness of the choices that exist in their lives and make positive changes that help them move from a trauma-centered life to a purposeful life, of which their child's circumstances are only a part. I asked Mary to share a few practical steps parents in this challenging situation can incorporate in their lives. As you consider these strategies, evaluate what you have in place in your life and what changes you may want to make to strengthen your ability to manage life successfully. Here are Mary's suggestions:

1. Connect. Difficult circumstances often lead to feelings of isolation. Friends and family who were initially supportive

fall away over time. Some who care deeply simply lack the time and energy to offer long-term support. For others, feelings of shame or embarrassment over their child's situation lead them to pull back from friends, family, and their faith community. First, a life-giving intimate connection with God and authentic community can make the difference between barely hanging on and experiencing God's purposes and peace in the midst of great pain and suffering. Next, cultivate community and build a diverse support team: church, small groups, experts, a coach, a cleaning service, friends who run errands for you, companions who make you laugh, even a hairdresser or manicurist. Be creative.

2. Identify and release your energy drains. Start by identifying drains in these areas: spiritual, emotional, mental health, finances, marriage, work, friends and community, church, home environment, and fun and leisure. Then identify what you can release or delegate to others. Ask yourself which items are essential for life and ruthlessly eliminate the "should do's" so you'll gain energy for the important things.

3. Alter negative self-talk. Listen for any self-defeating thoughts or internal messages and make a deliberate choice to realign your thoughts with God's Word. Read His Word daily, talk with a trusted friend, and surround yourself with people of faith.

4. Seek professional help when needed to facilitate healing from trauma, manage any depression or anxiety, rebuild a meaningful life amid life-altering circumstances, and engage God's purposes in the midst of pain.

No Matter What the Challenge May Be . . .

Our adult children are ultimately in charge of their lives, to the best of their capability. Our parental tasks are to understand the challenges they face and identify their capabilities, limitations, and opportunities (and ours as well) so we can plan effectively. Then we can work through our personal emotions, support our children as they deal with their own feelings, seek education and support for ourselves, and offer those resources to our children if they are open to suggestions.

> We must draw close to God and ask Him to calm our fears, heal our pain, and open the eyes of our heart so we can listen for His voice and follow His leading.

The most powerful step we can take to help us follow through on these tasks successfully is to ask God to fill us with His love and remind us that He loves our children and has a plan for their lives and for ours. Then we can move forward, confident He will guide our steps.

When my own children face trying times in their lives, I struggle because I want to rescue, fix, and heal. And yet I know that's not my role now. So I have found it most helpful if I envision partnering with God to care for them. Ultimately, He is their heavenly Father and He is in control. He has a plan for their lives and He asks them to seek Him, trust Him, and follow as He leads. He calls on me to be available when He wants to use me as an instrument to work in their lives. Sometimes that requires my active involvement in meeting needs, and sometimes it means taking time to work through my own feelings and educate myself so I'll be better prepared to assist when called upon. At other times it means I am to love, pray, and encourage my children as others step in to care for them—all the time trusting that He is in control.

As parents, we love our children and want to give them our

best care. So we must draw close to God and ask Him to calm our fears, heal our pain, and open the eyes of our heart so we can listen for His voice and follow His leading. When we place our trust in Him to guide us, He faithfully shows us how to love and care for our children with His amazing love—no matter what challenges life brings their way.

On a Personal Note

Is your child facing a difficult life challenge right now? If so, how are you supporting him? How are you taking care of yourself? What about other family members who may be impacted as well?

What resources are you drawing on that can provide education and support for you, perhaps for your child, and for other family members and caregivers?

Consider the tips given earlier in this chapter to identify strategies you can incorporate to help you effectively support your child and meet your own needs.

Ask God to help you find meaning and purpose in your life and in the life of your child as you both move through the challenges before you. Listen for His voice and look for His hand at work in your lives.

Helpful Resources

The following resources may prove helpful support for yourself, your child, and for other family members and caregivers dealing with major life challenges:

- *www.sarahorn.com*—resources for military wives and families

- *www.bluestarmothers.org*—nonprofit service organization for mothers who now have or have had children serving honorably in the military

- *www.newlifechristiancoaching.com*; *www.maryyerkes .com*—Mary J. Yerkes, Life Coaching for Christians and Chronic Illness Coaching

- *www.nami.org*—National Alliance on Mental Illness

- *www.disability.gov*—access to comprehensive disability-related information and resources

- *www.speakupforhope.org*—A nonprofit organization established by Carol and Gene Kent to provide hope to inmates and their families through encouragement and resources. Carol has also written out of the depths of her own life experiences to help parents adjust to difficult life changes and unwanted challenges, including the books *When I Lay My Isaac Down, A New Kind of Normal,* and *Between a Rock and a Grace Place.*

- *www.deborahdunn.com*—Deborah Dunn's focus is to help individuals, couples, and families build healthy relationships and heal wounded hearts.

- *www.settingboundaries.com*—Allison Bottke's ministry to parents whose adult children are struggling with difficult behaviors and also to adults who are caring for their aging parents. Information is based on her books *Setting Boundaries With Your Adult Children* and *Setting Boundaries With Your Aging Parents.*

- Celebrate Recovery groups—offered by many churches throughout the country as a ministry to their members and community. This program provides support for people who are struggling with a variety of hurts, habits, or hang-ups (compulsive behaviors). Its twelve-step program is based on Christian principles and centers around eight recovery principles based on the Beatitudes (found in the book of Matthew).

Chapter Nine

Give Yourself Some TLC

*"We cannot be a source of strength unless we nurture
our own strength."*
—M. SCOTT PECK, PSYCHIATRIST AND AUTHOR

Parenting is not a sprint; it's a marathon. Wouldn't you agree? So
if we want to finish the race well, we need to be in shape. Not only
that, statistics say we mid-lifers have many years yet ahead of us.
And while I want to be a great wife, a great parent to my children,
and the best grandmother I can be, I also want to enjoy everything
this season of my life has to offer. I want to laugh and play, to learn
and grow, to explore new things, and savor favorites. I want to fill
my life with music and enjoy the beauty of nature. I want times to
reach for the stars and other times to be still and reflect. I want to
share life with family and friends, perhaps even make new friends.
And I want to explore the ways I can serve God in this season of
my life. I know there will be some great times in the days ahead.
There will also be some challenges, and I want to be prepared to
meet those as well.

I know that if I'm going to accomplish those desires, I need
to be sure my body, mind, and spirit are ready. I need to take
care of myself if I want to live my best life, share it with those

I love, and support them when they need me. I love my family and friends, and I always want the best for them. When I take care of myself, I'm giving them the best wife, the best mother, the best friend, the best person I can give them for their lives. They benefit, and so do I. But when I don't tend to my needs, we all suffer.

What about you? What do you want for your life? What do you want to offer to those you care about and care for? What kind of shape are you in? Is it time, perhaps, for a little personal TLC?

Some parents are drained physically, emotionally, and perhaps financially, by the time their children reach adulthood. They wonder how they will take care of themselves and perhaps continue to meet their children's needs as well. If parents are run-down physically, they don't have the energy to be available when they want to step in and help out. If stressed out, they can't deal with their children's emotional struggles or provide support for their children. If parents have given and given financially, they may find their savings drained, leaving them unable to enjoy dreams they had for their own future. Even their spiritual lives may be impacted as they recognize the need for time to nurture their souls. Instead of experiencing pleasure, excitement, and anticipation, they feel disappointment, uncertainty, and perhaps exhaustion.

Then there are parents who assumed when their children reached adulthood, they would have more time to themselves, only to find they are stepping in more than they anticipated to help meet their children's needs. Their plans for this stage of life remain on hold as they wonder when or even if they will ever have time to follow their own dreams.

Some children have taken on the responsibilities of adulthood themselves and they no longer need direct support from their parents, leaving the children enjoying their independence and the parents wondering, "What am I supposed to do now? My identity has been wrapped up in my children for so long, I don't really know who I am or what I want out of this stage of my life. Even our marriage has been all about them. It's supposed to be a great time in life, but I feel like I've lost a part of me and I don't know where to go from here."

Do you find yourself relating to any of these groups? As parents, we want to have a good relationship with our adult children and support them in healthy ways, but we must also learn to manage our resources wisely so we can take care of both our marriage and ourselves. When we do so, we are in a better position physically, emotionally, and spiritually to know how and when to address our children's needs. While we want to be available to help as we can, we must realize we're also role models. As we take care of ourselves and take advantage of the opportunities God has given us to enjoy life, we are showing them that self-care is important. It's not a question of self-preservation or self-sacrifice. It's a matter of making time for both.

Jesus was the greatest example of one whose life was devoted to loving and serving others. There were times when He poured himself out to meet the needs of those who came to Him. Yet we read that there were also times when He went off alone to rest and pray. He knew the importance of restoring His physical and spiritual strength, and He modeled the need to renew ourselves so we can serve. If we want to be a vessel He can use to care for others, including our children, we must take care of our vessel and take time to refill it so we will indeed be useful.

Nurturing the Nurturer

A quote attributed to Frederick Buechner reminds us: "Love your neighbor as yourself, we're told. Maybe before I can love my neighbor very effectively, I have to love me—not in the sense of a blind passion but in the sense of looking after, of wishing well, of forgiving when necessary, of being my own friend."

> **This is not just a time to replenish our resources, it's also a time to enjoy life, savor the familiar, and explore the unknown.**

This is not just a time to replenish our resources, it's also a time to enjoy life, savor the familiar, and explore the unknown. This can be an active, growing, exciting time as we uncover all this stage of our lives has to offer. It's a time to dust off and perhaps even redefine the talents, desires, friendships, gifts, and curiosities we may have tucked aside as we raised our children. Now they're adults learning to take charge of their own lives. While we will want to assist with some of their needs, we can also devote time and resources to exploring this new season of our own lives and enjoying to the fullest all God has designed for us.

So if we are ready to focus on ourselves, where do we begin? Authors Janice Hanna and Kathleen Y'Barbo suggest aspects of our lives we can evaluate to help us make this life stage the best it can be. Their book *The House Is Quiet, Now What?* identifies areas to examine as we consider how we want to redefine ourselves and rediscover our dreams, desires, and talents. Take a look at their list and consider the possibilities that may be waiting for you to explore:

- Your relationship with God (Can you see it deepening over time?)

- Your self/your purpose (After all, we often don't know who we are at this stage.)

- Your marriage (Let the sparks fly!)

- Your time (You're liable to have more of it, and that's a good thing!)

- Your career (Hmmm. I wonder what I want to be when I grow up?)

- Your spiritual gifts (You have some, you know!)

- Your house (home remodeling)

- Your health (joining a gym and/or dieting)

- Your place in the body of Christ (service, missions)

- Your relationship with parents, siblings, and other family members

- Your friendships (both new friends and old)

- Learning a new skill (computers, photography, dance lessons, etc.)

- Hobbies (Yes! You finally have the time!)

- Volunteering (The possibilities are endless.)[1]

Yes, it's a big list, and it may suggest several changes you'd like to make for this season of your life. Are you uncertain about what to do? Overwhelmed by the number of things you'd like to address? Unsure about where or how to begin? The good news is this: You don't have to tackle it all today, and there's help available if you want someone to guide you in evaluating your desires and setting your goals.

Begin by allowing yourself to do a little personal inventory and ask: "How is my life going in this area? What goals do I want to set so I can enjoy it to the fullest and experience all God has in store for me?" Then you can plan the steps you'll take to follow those desires and fulfill those passions.

Making the Most of This Time—Parents Share Their Tips

I love this parenting quote attributed to Susan Savannah: "If your kids are giving you a headache, follow the directions on the aspirin bottle, especially the part that says, 'Keep away from children.'"

Whether our children give us pats on the back or headaches, we need to step away from their lives—at times—and take care of ourselves. Of course, we know we need to make certain our lives don't totally revolve around our children and grandchildren (if we are blessed with them). However, sometimes we don't know how to make that a reality in our everyday lives.

We also recognize that we must be in the best shape possible for those times when our children need us. I asked some friends how they are taking care of themselves so they can be the best parents and grandparents at this stage of their lives. Here are some of their responses. Perhaps they will spark some ideas as you consider how to give yourself a little TLC.

Nadine recognizes the value of sharing time with friends as a way to maintain her health and well-being:

> I think the fun things I do with friends such as playing cards (to promote brain activity and memory), traveling (spending time with friends and visiting new places), and Bible study (growing in the Lord together) are so important for this time in my life. Water aerobics has opened up another whole world for me. Not only does it help me stay fit, I've also met people I would never have met otherwise. We call it our water social club. I also enjoy volunteering for causes I've had an interest in and never got to do when my children were at home. I am busy, but never too busy that I cannot spend time with my grandkids. I try to keep a balance there. I am blessed to have the time and ability to enjoy all these things.

Linda and her husband are also focusing on maintaining good health, so they exercise together. "It's hard, but it's fun to work out with my husband," she says. "We want to be in the best shape we can be. We also enjoy traveling and even stepping out of our comfort zone in our small town to go visit other places nearby for dinner, dancing, the theatre, and special events. We want to explore new things together and enjoy this time in our lives."

Jill is a single mom facing some challenges with her adult son. She has learned that she can't carry the weight of her problems alone and she needs to understand the scope of her son's problems. So she attends a support group to educate herself about her son's addiction struggles and learn how to respond in a healthy way. "That group has been great for me," Jill shared. "It's a great place to vent, unwind, and understand what's going on with my son. I'm learning how to cope and finding a lot of strength through the support of others who understand my challenges. I think I am becoming a better parent to my son and taking better care of myself as well."

Parenting can take quite a toll on a marriage. So when a couple reaches the time when their children are grown, it's important to focus on enhancing their relationship: rekindling what might have been set aside, restoring what might have been a struggle, rediscovering each other, reconnecting to what's important in their relationship, and renewing their commitment to share life and love. Kris shares a few tips for doing those very things:

> John and I are enjoying lots of new things that we could never do when the kids were around. I love the spontaneity we can experience now. I will get a hotel room and not tell him until that evening, or reserve a table at a restaurant and make it a surprise. I will have candles on the table or eat dinner with china and crystal for no reason. I also make new dishes that are difficult but yummy. I think women (and men, too) often quit cooking when there are only two people.
>
> I think we have to work at making things interesting and

varied. Occasionally, I will leave a love note on his mirror and John has written me a note in soap that shows up with steam when I shower! I know how much I enjoy the adventures in life and I don't want them to stop.

Christine is the caregiver for her adult son and her sister. Both have chronic health issues and live in her home. Much of her time is devoted to their medical care and household needs, along with managing the finances and overseeing their family-owned business. She knows that to meet all those responsibilities and cope with the stress that comes with the challenges, she must take care of herself, emotionally as well as physically.

> Social networks are important outlets for me. I enjoy connecting with friends through community organizations, and I volunteer in a local ministry that provides opportunity for me to use my talents to help others. I also enjoy the convenience of e-mail and Facebook to stay in touch with family and friends. All these things energize me and lift my spirits so I can do my best to meet the challenges at this time of my life. They are the best medicine.

When I asked Patti to comment about how she is taking care of herself at this life stage, she laughed:

> I'm busier than I ever thought I'd be, but I am enjoying so many things. My husband and I attend our grandchildren's sports games as well as their school and church performances, which is fun for the grandchildren and great time together for the two of us. They are very active, so we are on the go a lot. We used to feel we had to go to everything they were part of, but we are now learning to pace ourselves and even say no sometimes. I'm also teaching a Bible study group and attending another one, enjoying more time to study God's Word with other women. And of course, Bill and I like to watch sports on TV together, so we catch

whatever games we can. I also get together with some friends for a "girls' night out" once a month, which is always fun.

I know it sounds like I'm busy . . . I am! I think being active and having fun is important for me, and it's also a good model for my children, as long as I take care of myself in the process. I know that I won't always be able to continue this pace, but until the time comes when I'm forced to slow down, I'll continue to stay busy—to grow spiritually through study, enjoy my grandkids, and enjoy time with my husband.

These friends are taking important steps to live life to the fullest. They are learning how to accept and incorporate the changes and challenges taking place in their lives as they consider both their opportunities and their limitations. They are making intentional choices to honor their passion, exercise their talents and abilities, strengthen their relationships, and bring joy to their journey. They are also realizing an important principle that can guide us through life's ups and downs: We must pay attention to our attitude. The attitude we choose to take on will determine much of the way in which we live the rest of our lives. It will impact our health, our relationships, our opportunities, our challenges, even our relationship with God. And while we cannot control everything in our lives, we can control the attitude we choose to embrace, so let us choose with care.

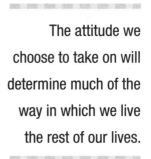

The attitude we choose to take on will determine much of the way in which we live the rest of our lives.

A Promise From Your Heavenly Father

When we wonder where we will get the strength to accomplish our goals and how we can be all God wants us to be in these days filled with so many challenges, we will do best to pause and remember a promise the prophet Isaiah shared. He spoke about God's provision for His children: "He gives strength to the weary and increases the power of the weak . . . Those who hope in the Lord will renew their strength. They will soar on wings like eagles; they will run and not grow weary, they will walk and not be faint" (Isaiah 40:29, 31).

> God wants us to do our best to take care of ourselves so we can fully embrace the life He designed for each of us and be vessels He can use to pour out His love, His grace, and His goodness into the lives of our children.

God wants us to do our best to take care of ourselves so we can fully embrace the life He designed for each of us and be vessels He can use to pour out His love, His grace, and His goodness into the lives of our children. The apostle Paul understood this challenge. "Therefore, I urge you, brothers and sisters, in view of God's mercy, to offer your bodies as living sacrifices, holy and pleasing to God—this is your true and proper worship. Do not conform to the pattern of this world, but be transformed by the renewing of your mind. Then you will be able to test and approve what God's will is—his good, pleasing and perfect will" (Romans 12:1–2).

On a Personal Note

What steps are you currently taking to care for yourself physically? Emotionally? Spiritually?

How are you balancing both the need to care for yourself and the desire to respond to your children's needs?

What areas need your attention?

What steps are you willing to take that will help you live your life to the fullest and experience all God has planned for you?

What will you do to give yourself a little TLC each day? Why not begin today?

If you want to incorporate some of the suggestions in this chapter into your life but are not sure how to do so, consider consulting with a counselor or life coach who can help you explore how to take steps to nurture yourself and enjoy all that life has to offer while also caring for the needs of those around you.

Chapter Ten

Leave a Positive Footprint

"Each day of our lives we make deposits in the memory banks of our children."
—CHARLES R. SWINDOLL, *THE STRONG FAMILY*

I come from a long line of hardworking, God-fearing Irish men and women who left their native soil as young adults and ventured across the Atlantic in search of new beginnings. They carried with them determination, courage, faith, the love of family, and a heritage rich with the music and legends of their homeland. Their stories, music, laughter, and teachings were woven into the fabric of my life—priceless gifts that warm my heart as their Irish brogue resonates in my memory.

They were strict, no doubt, with definite views of the world and how I was to find my way in it. Life was not always serious, however. They worked hard to provide for their families while also making time to share meals and lively conversation about life in "the ol' country." Oh, the tales they could tell about growing up in Ireland—and with such straight faces. I sometimes had trouble distinguishing what was truth and what was . . . a little blarney, shall we say?

Lessons From My Heritage

Now that I have my own children and a new grandchild, I recognize even more the value of sharing stories and passing along snapshots of my heritage. As parents, we tried to be sure our children knew right from wrong. We encouraged them to do well in school, be well rounded and well dressed, and to be polite to their elders. We did our best to care for their needs as we helped them prepare to manage life on their own. We may now be doing some of those things for our grandchildren.

But what about our legacy? What are we leaving to those who will follow us, besides heirlooms, photographs, and a savings account? Our role is to help our children (and the generations to come) value the experiences that have shaped our lives and the lessons we've learned along the way.

I'm grateful for family members who shared time together to ponder life, to laugh and cry, to dream and hope. I learned much from them as a child and now my husband and I have the privilege of fulfilling that role in the lives of our children and their children.

A Grandfather's Gift

As my grandfather enjoyed the evening of his life, he decided it was important to make certain his children and grandchildren were prepared for whatever troubles life might bring. He knew struggles and unexpected challenges would come along, and he couldn't protect us from every harmful experience. But he wanted us to be prepared in case we met with a particular menace. So he set out on a mission. He scoured the grounds around his home for the perfect wood. Not just any stick would do. He carefully selected one for each of us and lovingly trimmed each piece, shaping it into the perfect tool. When he was satisfied with his handiwork, he presented each of us with our gift—a shillelagh. Mine has its place—at my grandfather's specific direction—in my living room near the fireplace. Its purpose is too ward off any leprechauns that might be lurking. You see, he believed (or at least he convinced me that he believed) leprechauns are not to be trusted. They are the "little people" who come out at night, full of mischief and ready to stir up trouble. He wanted to be certain that before he died, he prepared his loved ones to protect their homes and families. He wanted to pass on a part of his heritage. He didn't lecture or force his viewpoints on us. He simply shared his beliefs. Then with an Irish chuckle and a twinkle in his eye, he left it to us to decide how to respond. I have kept the stick as a reminder, not so much about leprechauns, but rather about my grandfather's love for his family.

Grandpop shared from his past through a gift that reflected his beliefs.

A Mother's Actions

My mother was a quiet woman—gentle in spirit and unwavering in her faith, even in the most challenging, painful times. While she shared with me a few stories about her childhood, she kept much of her life tucked carefully and privately in her memory and in her heart. And yet, as I reflect, I realize much of the legacy she passed along to me came through her actions.

Mom openly—and authentically—lived what she believed. She studied her Bible and spent time each day in prayer. She taught little children at church about God's love for them. She made certain the coffeepot was ready and always had something sweet in the pantry, just in case someone dropped by for a visit. She counseled women who were struggling as wives and mothers to seek God's wisdom for their lives. She sacrificed herself for those she loved. She cared for my father during his many illnesses. She battled cancer as long as she could, and then she prepared for the Lord to take her to be with Him.

The legacy she passed down was clear: Love God. Obey Him. Serve Him. Follow wherever He leads. Trust Him with your whole heart and hold on to His promises, no matter what life brings. The mantle has now fallen on me to honor that legacy in my own life and to pass the wisdom I've gleaned from her on to my children and theirs.

Mom shared the faith that was the foundation of her life through her actions.

Parents' Words

When we found out we were going to become grandparents, my husband and I began a journal for our son and daughter-in-law. During the months we waited for the birth of their little one, we recorded thoughts about parenting. Things that went well. Funny stories and precious memories. Struggles we had. Truths we discovered along the way. Lessons God taught us. Wisdom we gained. We wanted to pass on part of our past—our heritage—to our children as they prepared to step into the role of parents.

We shared our experiences and our encouragement through our written words.

Our Footprint

We tend to think of the inheritance we are passing down primarily in terms of property, material possessions, finances, or bequests that are made in a will. But the legacy we create also includes the personal aspects of our lives—our character. The beliefs we profess, the values we live by, the priorities we establish, the choices we make, and the way we treat others, all form the essence of our unique character, which is also part of our legacy. Each of these qualities has a powerful influence on the lives of those we love. It is part of our footprint that will impact them long after we are gone. A part of my family heritage was passed down by my grandfather through a gift, my mother through her actions, and my husband and me through our written words. Each one is a legacy wrapped in love.

Whether we realize it or not, as parents, we've been building that legacy since the day our children were born, and we continually shape that footprint each day. They've watched how we've lived life and determined whether or not they will embrace the patterns we've set or choose their own course. They've listened to what we've taught them about what we believe in and what we've deemed as right and wrong. Even more so, they've watched how we applied those teachings in our own lives. Hopefully, we recognized that principle while our children were young and did all we could to live in a way that reflected our values and honored God's desires for us.

> **We have a fresh opportunity to influence the legacy we will pass along to them through the choices we now make for our own lives and through conversations we have with them, adult-to-adult.**

Now that our children are grown, many parents believe our years of influence have come to an end as our children—now adults—are making their own choices about how they want to live life. Some parents look back with satisfaction, some with regret, and most of us with a combination of both as we consider the impact we've made on the lives of our children. We wonder if the door of opportunity to make a positive impression has closed. But it's not too late, and there are many things we can still do to leave a lasting footprint on their lives.

Our adult children are taking on new roles and responsibilities, and they may look to us for counsel or observe more keenly how we are managing our own adult lives. We have a fresh opportunity to influence the legacy we will pass along to them through the choices we now make for our own lives and through conversations we have with them, adult-to-adult.

Authentic Living

Our own personal character is a powerful influence in the lives of our children and will be remembered for generations to come. They listen as we speak and watch as we react to life experiences, looking for congruency between our values and life choices—between our words and our actions. They compare how we treat them with how we treat others. If we reflect positive values consistently, we foster a sense of security that becomes the basis for their trust in us. So we need to be clear about our principles of right and wrong, and be certain our lives reflect those values. We must live with integrity.

We need to speak and conduct ourselves in a way that draws our family toward us, encouraging them to feel loved and safe. That means we need to be careful how we express (and manage) our emotions, including how we respond when we disagree with them or when they disappoint us. Do we encourage them or do we criticize? Do we condemn and put stumbling blocks in their way? As we speak the truth, we need to do so grounded in love and focused on building up rather than tearing down.

It's also important for us to be careful how we handle victory and how we react to defeat, as both situations reflect our character. And what about our attitude? As we look at life, do we see a glass half empty or one half full?

When we live authentic lives with character that is based on

God's principles, our children will be more likely to draw close to us. When they feel loved and respected, they will be more open to consider our values, respect our actions, and understand our hearts. When they trust us, they will be more apt to allow their children to share life with us. When they see us model the approach to life we want for them, they will be more likely to consider our words of encouragement and counsel.

> When our children see us making wise decisions, managing life's challenges effectively, living authentically, and creating stability in our lives, they will be more apt to seek our counsel.

If we seek God's guidance and do all we can to live in a manner that honors Him and reflects His truths, we will create a legacy of love, joy, peace, patience, kindness, goodness, faithfulness, gentleness, and self-control—fruit of His Spirit. When our children see us making wise decisions, managing life's challenges effectively, living authentically, and creating stability in our lives, they will be more apt to seek our counsel or reflect on our lives as a positive reference when they face their own challenges. They may not always make the same choices, but they will have seeds of positive influence planted in their minds and hearts that can flow from generation to generation.

Our Spiritual Legacy

When we share our spiritual beliefs with our children and grandchildren through our conversation and through our own daily living, we have opportunity to pass along a spiritual legacy to them as well. We can teach powerful lessons as we share about our relationship with God and how we've worked through our own spiritual struggles. I remember as a young child watching my mother face some challenging times. I sometimes wondered how she could hold on and press through difficulties she faced when many women would have given up. She was quiet about many aspects of her life, but open and honest about her love for God, her understanding of Him, and her trust in His faithfulness. She didn't waver, and I watched as God faithfully cared for her.

Even if our children choose to set aside our spiritual influence and follow a different path, we can hold on to hope as we demonstrate our faithfulness to God and our desire to live lives that are pleasing to Him. We don't need to preach, we don't need to condemn, and we don't need to give up hope. We do need to hold fast to the spiritual truths that guide our lives and ask God to let His light shine through.

Our Finances and Possessions

I was blessed with a very wise and loving mother-in-law, and my husband and I always enjoyed time with her. We lived in another state so our visits were not as frequent as we would have liked, but time with her was always special. As she approached her later years, she began to give things away to family members. Often, as we prepared to leave after a visit, she would choose something to send home with us. "Here, go ahead and take this now. I want you to have it." A vase. A photo album. An afghan she had made. She enjoyed sharing with those she loved things that had been a part of her life.

My mother was like that as well, especially when she realized her life would be coming to a close sooner than she had expected. She spent many hours with me, talking about things she wanted to pass on to certain family members and friends. And she took steps to personally pass many of her possessions along to those she loved while she could do so in person.

The material things both women possessed were not of great financial value, but they were part of the life and heritage of these women. They wanted to share that legacy with their children and grandchildren. As parents, we need to consider how we will pass on material things and financial resources to our children and grandchildren.

One way we can do that is by writing a will that specifies how we want our possessions and finances handled when we are gone. It is important to clarify how we want to distribute our inheritance so it will be a blessing to them and not a burden. We must do our best to make fair and thoughtful decisions that will help encourage a healthy working relationship among our children as they carry out our wishes.

It is especially helpful if we share information about the arrangements we wish to make—along with our priorities, desires, and plans—so we can avoid surprises that will create problems for our children later on. Our children need to know where our wills and important papers are stored and who will take the lead in managing our estate when we are gone. We do need to use discretion as to when and how we share this information, respecting the needs and concerns of family members.

There are times when parents need professional assistance in taking special needs into consideration. For example, my friend Megan has a handicapped daughter and she wants to make arrangements for her continued care, so consequently, her funds might not be equally disbursed among her children. With the help of an attorney, a financial planner, and a medical consultant, she is setting aside a portion of her funds for her daughter's care, with the remainder to be divided equally among her other children. She gathered her children to share her intentions and plan so they would understand that she was providing for the care of their sibling to avoid their having to carry that financial responsibility.

Julie has three grown sons, and one of them is living a lifestyle that has troubled her and her husband greatly. They love their son but do not want to contribute to his destructive choices, so they have set clear guidelines in their wills about how their finances are to be distributed. They appointed someone outside the family to manage their estate and shared their plan with their sons so all are aware of their desires and concerns.

When it comes to our financial legacy, we need to consider how we can honor our values, reflect our priorities and our character, and consider our children's needs. Some people identify a portion of their funds to be given to their church or an organization, and some establish trust funds for specific needs, such as education for their children or grandchildren. Some parents gift part of their financial resources to family members and charities while they are still living. There are certain tax laws that must be considered, so consulting a financial advisor may be helpful. No matter how much or how little you have to pass on and what choices you make about how you want to do so, it is important to plan carefully and responsibly and establish clear guidelines for carrying out your plan.

It's Not Just About the Gift

Passing on a positive financial legacy is not only about determining how possessions or funds will be distributed. It also includes demonstrating wise financial choices and planning. We can let our children and grandchildren know how our values impact our financial decisions and what steps we take to be good stewards of what God has provided. We can teach them through our example how to tithe, how to share what we have, how to make decisions carefully, how to consider the needs of others, how to plan and budget, how to honor our values and establish priorities, how to sacrifice, and even how to seek help when needed.

Rhonda and her husband found a program that has helped them effectively manage their finances, so they offered to purchase the same program for their newly married adult son and his wife—no pressure, just an invitation, if the young couple would like to try it out.

> As we make wise choices, we model for our children and grandchildren how to be financially responsible, and we help prepare them for the time when we will pass along an inheritance to them.

When my husband and I stepped into a new phase of our lives, we sat down with our children and talked about the decisions we were considering, including downsizing, a move, job changes, and some financial shifts. We wanted them to have an overall view of the factors we were considering, how we were approaching the decisions before us, and the impact our choices would have on them. It set the stage for understanding other choices that have come along since those initial changes. Since that open discussion, we've had follow-up conversations about our future financial planning. They have also talked about their own financial goals and plans. It has strengthened mutual respect, understanding, and even a level of accountability as we are now following through on the decisions we made and plans we established.

As parents, we need to be continually aware that as we make wise choices, we model for our children and grandchildren how to be financially responsible and we help prepare them for the time when we will pass along an inheritance to them. We gift them with a strong financial legacy to build upon.

Traditions and Memories

My older son was about four years old and my younger son two at the time. I was gone for the afternoon and my husband was enjoying time with the boys. I'm not quite sure whose idea it was, and all three of them deny conjuring up the plan. I just know I came home to find the coffee table perched up on the sofa with the cushions on the floor in front of it, two little boys sliding head first down the "coffee table slide," and Dad taking pictures in between the cheers and laughter. There was an immediate hush as three sets of eyes looked at me with that are-we-in-trouble? look. What could I say? What could I do except enjoy the moment that has proven to be one of our family's most fun memories? In fact, we have that coffee table in the attic, ready to pass down to grandchildren who will someday enjoy their daddy's first slide.

As we think about money, possessions, values, and life lessons we want to pass along to our children, let's also consider the legacy we will leave in terms of family traditions and memories. While the coffee table event was a long time ago, the best part of the memory is the conversations we've had through the years about an unexpected playful adventure. Take time to talk about the special events and the everyday experiences you've shared—the fun of vacation trips together, the laughter while exchanging silly gifts or practical jokes, the special times cooking in the kitchen or playing in the yard, the pride of accomplishments, the pain of grief, the sympathy shared in struggles, and the joy shared in victories.

Carolyn loves scrapbooking, so she organized her family photos and assembled them into albums for each child. She included notes about the emotions that were shared with the experiences captured in the pictures. She has not given the collections to her children yet but has them easily accessible so they can look through the pages of their past when they come to visit. She says it spurs great conversation when they get together, which then generates more laughter, more photos, and more memories. You may want to consider scanning your photos and downloading them onto CDs so each family member can have a complete set.

Some families have researched their heritage and drawn a family tree with accompanying stories about their ancestors. Libraries, the Internet, and older family members are great sources of information to help you with such a project. Once you've pulled together the information, create booklets or computer files you can share with your children and grandchildren. You may also want to consider compiling written notes about some of the special items you've acquired through the years and perhaps write stories about your life to share with your children and grandchildren.

My friend Patricia has written letters to her grandchildren for special occasions in their lives. She penned her thoughts about what they may be experiencing, stories from her own childhood, words of encouragement, and advice that she wants them to have as they grow up. Each child has a special keepsake box with the sealed letters waiting to be opened on their special days.

Now that our children are adults, it may be time to begin passing the torch when it comes to some family traditions. They may want to have a holiday dinner at their house instead of always coming to ours. They may want us to share old family recipes so they can learn to prepare the special meals they enjoyed growing up. Or they may want to create their own menu instead of serving the traditional family fare. We may be at a place where we need to let go of some responsibilities and ask them to step in to take over. We may even find we need to set aside some traditions and establish new ones that take into account their interests, needs, priorities, schedules, and finances, all of which may differ from ours.

As I adjust to changes in our growing family, I have to remind myself that when I was a young adult, my parents had to make some shifts in traditions and expectations to fit with my life, particularly when I married and had children of my own. It's important for us as parents to be open, understanding, flexible, honest if we have concerns, and willing to work with them to find the best way of sharing family time together.

> May the legacies we pass on be ones that will be pleasing to God and helpful to our children and grandchildren as they embrace whatever their futures hold.

We give many things to our children through the years. May we ask God to guide our minds and our hearts and grant us wisdom as we consider not just what we are doing for them but also what we are instilling in them through our words, our actions, and gifts. May the legacies we pass on be ones that will be pleasing to God and helpful to our children and grandchildren as they embrace whatever their futures hold.

On a Personal Note

Set aside some time to focus on each of these areas of your life. And consider the footprint you are creating that will be a legacy to pass along to your children and those who will follow them. Perhaps you will want to write down your thoughts about each of these aspects of your legacy: moral, emotional, spiritual, financial, traditions, and memories.

- Begin by asking God to show you His desires for your life and the legacy He wants to reflect through you.

- As you consider each of these areas, what would you like to pass along?

- What goals would you like to set?

- Do you need assistance to help clarify the best ways to achieve your goals?

- What will you begin doing today to address the desires of your heart and create a footprint that you want to pass along to those you love?

Chapter Eleven

Offer Resources—When the Door Is Open

*"A wise parent humors the desire for independent action,
so as to become the friend and advisor
when his absolute rule shall cease."*
—ELIZABETH GASKELL, NOVELIST

While our adult children want to make their own choices and handle their own affairs, they often need assistance with information and resources. And they need referrals for purchases, repairs, services, and consultants for various life management tasks such as insurance coverage, financial management, and medical care. Sometimes they come to us and ask, "Can you help me with ____?" Other times, they come with a request for direction, "Who should I go to about ____?" Then there are times when we see them facing a need, and they've communicated their desire to handle it on their own. But we know they are uncertain about what to do. We want to help, yet we know we can't take charge. So how can we respond in a respectful way?

We can be ready with advice or assistance if they ask, and we can have resources available if the door is open for information and suggestions. The Internet has opened countless doors to insight and "how to's" for almost any problem we encounter. It may be helpful for us to have resources on hand—tip sheets, Web site addresses, business cards, and contact information for local assistance—to pass along when appropriate and welcomed. Some children will ask for the information; others want to secure it on their own. You'll need to assess each child individually and respond accordingly. Don't impose. Just be aware and ready if assistance is requested. I found that one of my sons asked for some guidance about a particular issue and the other wanted to research it for himself. If the door is open and the need present, you may find an opportunity to share information in a casual manner without a lecture. For example, if you give your child an appliance or tool, you might want to mention briefly how you care for yours. "Here's something that might come in handy. I find mine works best if I _____." Or, "I bank at _____ and think the services and rates are good. You might want to check them out."

> **Don't impose. Just be aware and ready if assistance is requested.**

I am including a few tools you may want to have on hand if your child asks for information as he sets up his own living space and takes on full responsibility for the care of his possessions, home, vehicle, finances, and overall well-being. You may find them helpful for yourself as well.

Home Organization Tips

Certified Professional Organizer Ellen Delap offers tips we can pass along to our children as they set up their own homes. Her suggestions can be useful to us also as we reorganize after our children move out. Here are four steps she recommends we implement ourselves or share with our children. If you share them, do so with the proper phrasing, timing, and suggestions that are comfortable and appropriate for your particular child:

Creating order in a new home establishes a baseline as we step out into the world. It is in setting a serene and nurturing spot for us to depart from and return to daily that we feel best about who we are and what we accomplish. When I work with people moving into new living arrangements, reorganizing after a child moves away, or helping parents as they downsize, these four steps prove to be important guides for reorganization:

Step 1: De-clutter. Do all you can to de-clutter *before* you move into your new space if possible. It saves money on moving, time unpacking, and personal energy. De-clutter as you unpack, if you cannot do so prior to moving.

- De-cluttering closets can be one of the most difficult areas. Choose clothes that will transition you to your next lifestyle. Eliminate through consignment or donation those that do not make you look or feel fabulous in your new role.

- Bathrooms harbor lots of old cosmetics, toiletries, and travel items. Toss these if they are more than one year old.

- Often there is an overabundance of linens, kitchen utensils, and other household items. Choose what you use and pare down on duplication.

- Keepsakes and memorabilia are a very challenging area to de-clutter. Rather than stress a quantity, remember to honor what you are keeping. An item is honored in how it is kept and how it is specially stored or displayed. It also helps to define a boundary or location for these items, such as choosing an attractive and appropriate-size bin to keep these in or a certain shelf unit on which to display them. Keep only what is useful, functional, and loved.

- Papers can be overwhelming! Refer to Oprah.com for the *ABC's of Important Papers* on what to keep and for how long.

Step 2: Organize your living space.

- Start with your vision of your new space. What adjectives describe it? Think about what your needs are now and for the next five years. How do you want your space to look?

- Focus in on function. Determine how each room/space is used. Some rooms may have multiple uses, so think in terms of sections of the room. Once use is designated, determine the tools needed for what is done in the room and the storage for tools in that room.

- Next, consider your personal style reflected in your preferred modality. For example, visual people need to see all their clothes, so clothes are all hung on hangers.

- Think about your personal routines. Where does your laundry "drop"? This is where a sorter needs to be placed.

- Your organization needs to start in general, and then become customized to your personal style.

Step 3: Manage paper. Sometimes it is good to recognize obstacles to organization. Paper is especially challenging and overwhelming with the tsunami of paper that everyone receives every day. It's important to manage it wisely, keeping in mind such things as the link between paying bills on time and a good credit score, which helps with financial management.

- Create a command center for mail and papers to be sorted daily. It can be a small desktop sorter with categories: Action, Pay, and File.

- Start simple and small with a portable file box. Use hanging files with simple categories, such as Paid bills, Home, Car, Personal, and Work.

- Papers are best handled in small amounts, so find the means that best fits your lifestyle. For some it is a daily activity, and for others, once a week suffices.

Step 4: Create routines. Excellent systems are not enough. Routines provide the everyday aspect of organizing, from putting things back in place to the flow of events for a day or a week. Some adults naturally create routines while others find it challenging. Be open-minded and find what fits best for you, keeping in mind that what works for one person may not work for another. Having a good morning, evening, daily, weekly or monthly routine can make all the difference.

For more information, visit Ellen's Web site—*www.professional-organizer.com.*

Emergency and First Aid Preparedness

Every living space needs basic emergency, first aid, and repair kits in the event of a problem. We often don't think of these items until we face a situation and need to respond. You may want to assemble various kits you can pass along or give your child a list of suggestions so he can gather his own materials.

When it comes to general home maintenance, consider putting together a kit with basic tools for home and car repair—a hammer, screwdrivers, pliers, wrenches, nails, picture hangers, tape measure, level, glue, and tape. There are a variety of tool kits already assembled with a special design for both men and women available at stores selling tools and hardware. Or you can personalize a kit with your own preferences.

Every home and vehicle should have basic first aid materials on hand in the event of an emergency. First aid kits can be purchased at most pharmacies or through organizations such as the

American Red Cross. You can also assemble them on your own. You may want to tailor kits to specific needs such as for the home, car, boat, or for camping, bicycling, or hiking. I put together a basic kit that includes assorted bandages, cloth tape, dressing pads (for small wounds), small scissors, tweezers, antibiotic ointment, antiseptic wipes, hydrocortisone ointment, cold compress, aspirin, thermometer, other medications as required, and basic emergency first aid information.

If you've ever experienced a power outage or dealt with extreme weather conditions, such as tornados, hurricanes, floods, or other serious storms, you know the value of emergency response tools to help prior, during, and after a storm. You may want to recommend your child gather items together so he'll be prepared. Items our family has found helpful in times like these include: flashlight, battery-operated radio, battery-operated clock, extra batteries, drinking water, an extra set of car keys stored in a place easily accessible near an exit, an escape ladder if on a second floor, and an emergency response evacuation plan. You may want to recommend other items you find helpful to have on hand.

In the event of an emergency, it's important to quickly locate items such as cell phone and charger, important papers, purse/billfold, keys, emergency contact information, extra clothes, water, food, medications, personal hygiene items, clothing, and baby or pet supplies if appropriate. I've found it helpful to make a checklist of these things ahead of time because in an emergency you need to act quickly, and it may be difficult to think about everything that is needed.

A basic sewing kit is useful for quick repairs. These can be found at fabric stores or discount stores where sewing notions are sold. You can also gather items such as needles, straight pins, safety pins, basic colors of thread, scissors, and hem tape to form your own sewing kit.

Car Care Tips

As our adult children learn to manage life independently, they are also assuming responsibility for the maintenance of their vehicles. As they grew up, some helped their parents take care of the family vehicles and learned a few things along the way. Others saw their parents turn directly to mechanics for maintenance and repairs.

Our children must now learn about routine car care and how to identify problems that need attention. Some will ask us for help or instruction, while others want to handle things on their own. Even if they have someone else take care of their car's maintenance, they should have a basic understanding of what to request and what to expect for proper care. We can be available to give advice if they ask and offer to show them what to do if we have that knowledge. We can also provide information and referrals to help them learn on their own about basic care.

Jody DeVere, CEO of AskPatty.com, provides basic car care education and resources for consumers (particularly women) on car buying, selling, repair, care, and safety. Her site offers a variety of maintenance information that may be helpful to our children—both male and female—and to us. Here are some tips from Jody's Web site that may serve as a guide if you talk to your children about caring for their vehicles. Or you may simply want to pass the information along for their consideration.

"Ten Basic Car Care Tips to Improve Safety and Reliability"[1]

Some things as basic as checking the oil can go a long way toward improving the safety and reliability of your vehicle, plus it helps avoid costly repairs down the road. The Car Care Council recommends ten basic maintenance procedures to keep your car operating at its best:

1. Check the oil, filters, and fluids. Oil should be checked at every fill-up, and for maximum engine life, it should be changed per the owner's manual recommended intervals or every three months or 3,000 miles. Brakes, transmission, power steering, coolant, and windshield washer fluids should also be checked regularly. Your car's filters, including those for the transmission, fuel system, and interior ventilation, need regular inspection and replacement.

2. Inspect hoses at each oil change and have them replaced when leaking, brittle, cracked, rusted, swollen, or restricted. Check V-belts and serpentine belts for looseness and condition, and have them replaced when cracked, frayed, glazed, or showing signs of excessive wear. Typically replace the timing belt between 60,000 and 90,000 miles or the interval specified in the owner's manual to avoid a breakdown or serious engine damage.

3. Check the brake system every year and have the brake linings, rotors, and drums inspected at each oil change.

4. Check to be sure the battery connection is clean, tight, and corrosion-free. The battery should be tested regularly and replaced if necessary. (The average battery life is about five years if maintained properly. The replacement interval depends on your driving habits and conditions, battery type, and manufacturer's guidelines. Read the battery replacement interval guidelines that came with your battery or in the owner's manual.)

5. Inspect the exhaust system for leaks, damage, and broken

supports, or hangers if there is an unusual noise. Exhaust leaks can be dangerous and must be corrected without delay.

6. Schedule an engine performance maintenance interval (referred to as a tune-up for cars prior to 1981), which will help the engine deliver the best balance of power and fuel economy and produce the lowest level of emissions. Interval guidelines are found in your owner's manual.

7. Check the car's heating, ventilating, and air-conditioning (HVAC) system as proper heating and cooling performance is critical for interior comfort and for safety reasons, such as defrosting. Refer to your owner's manual for the proper maintenance intervals for each of these.

8. Inspect the steering and suspension system annually, including shock absorbers and struts, and chassis parts, such as ball joints, tie-rod ends, and other related components.

9. Check the pressure of all tires, including the spare, at least once a month. Check the tread for uneven or irregular wear and cuts and bruises along the sidewalls. Have your car's alignment checked at least annually to reduce tire wear and improve fuel economy and handling.

10. Test exterior and interior lights and have bulbs that are not working checked immediately. Replace windshield wiper blades every six months or when cracked, cut, torn, streaking, or chattering for optimum wiping performance and safety.

For more information, visit *www.AskPatty.com,* refer to your car's maintenance guide, or consult with a trusted mechanic.

Meal Planning

As our children move out of our home and into their own living spaces, they will assume responsibility for filling their own pantry, preparing their own meals, doing their laundry and cleaning. When it comes to meal preparation, you might consider giving a gift from the vast array of cookbooks and Web sites that target cooking for one or two, preparing quick meals, basic cooking techniques, and menu ideas for various tastes and special occasions. Books, utensils, cookware, gift cards to stores that carry home goods, and recipe cards with family favorites are great gifts for anyone, especially someone moving into a new living space. Of course, gift cards to local restaurants are also welcome treats.

> They should be offered as gifts or suggestions, with no pressure to use them and no strings attached.

Remember, you are offering tools and resources for them to *consider,* if they want to use them. They should be offered as gifts or suggestions, with no pressure to use them and no strings attached. Just as you've had opportunity to learn and then tweak the recipes and tips you've collected, now your children can take those ideas, give them their personal spin, and make them their own.

Budget Worksheet

Sound financial management is a vital part of anyone's success as an adult. While we should not meddle in our children's finances or direct how they should spend and save their money, we can offer assistance in a nonthreatening way. If the door is open to general conversation about finances, you may want to consider sharing a budget worksheet that can serve as a general guide.

If you choose to offer tips, worksheets, or referral information, clarify that you are simply passing along information for them to consider, not attempting to direct them in their choices. Do not ask them to reveal personal information. Be willing to discuss or share advice only if asked. Some parents have found financial management programs to be helpful tools personally and have passed those programs along to their children. If you draw up a suggested budget guide, here are categories you will want to include:

Income—gross income minus income taxes and other payroll deductions, leaving a balance of spendable income

Home expenses—mortgage or rent; insurance; property taxes; repairs; HOA or property management dues; amount set aside for home improvement

Utilities—electricity; water and sewer; gas; telephone; cable; Internet

Food—groceries; eating out; snacks

Health and medical—insurance; out-of-pocket; fitness

Family care—child care; child support

Transportation—car payments; gasoline; maintenance; license and inspections; insurance; tolls; public transportation; money set aside for future repairs

Clothing

Household products and toiletries

Grooming—hair; nails; skin care; makeup

Student loans

Credit cards

Other loans

Hobbies

Subscriptions

Vacations

Gifts

Pets—food; boarding; grooming; vet exams

Church tithes and offerings

Charitable contributions

Savings

Emergency fund

Have a place on the worksheet to record budgeted amounts and actual expenses/income for a month at a time so your child can assess how finances are flowing and what areas need adjustment. Some budget worksheets also have a place to identify when bills are due so those payments can be tracked as well. Once again, some children will know how to put something like this together on their own, while others may appreciate the guide to work from.

Additional Resources

Consider your child's unique lifestyle, needs, and desires. Then gather additional information that might be of assistance: Web site links, brochures, business cards from local businesses, articles you find on the Internet or in print, referrals for health care, insurance and legal assistance, and financial information.

Another great resource for your child would be a list of family members' birthdays, home and e-mail addresses, telephone numbers, and dates of special occasions. You might also suggest they take photos of their possessions and store them in a place outside their living space, in the event of theft or a natural disaster such as fire. Information on identify-theft prevention would be helpful to pass along as well.

Gather the various resource materials you want to share and assemble them into a packet or electronic file so you will have the materials available if your children ask for assistance. Preface your offering with the comment that you are simply passing along information that might be a helpful resource. A personal "how-to" guide—*with no strings attached.*

Remember, our role as parents of adult children is to be available with insight and information when they request such, with an attitude of confidence in their ability to learn how to manage life's challenges, with prayers that God will grant them wisdom and guidance, and with words of encouragement as they take charge of their lives.

> Be available with insight and information when your children request such, with an attitude of confidence in their ability to learn how to manage life's challenges, with prayers that God will grant them wisdom and guidance, and with words of encouragement as they take charge of their lives.

On a Personal Note

Consider your child's present life circumstances: living space, finances, interests and hobbies, transportation, eating habits, job, possessions, and health.

What information, resources, and tools would help him manage the various aspects of his life effectively?

What could you reasonably offer to assist him? How can you do so in a way that respects his independence and communicates confidence in his ability to take care of his life?

Chapter Twelve

Keep the Welcome Mat Out

"Family. We were a strange little band of characters trudging
through life, sharing diseases and toothpaste, coveting one
another's desserts, hiding shampoo, borrowing money, locking
each other out of our rooms, inflicting pain and kissing to heal
it in the same instant, loving, laughing, defending, and trying
to figure out the common thread that bound us all together."
—ERMA BOMBECK, HUMORIST

I nestled into a comfy chair on the back porch to enjoy a fresh cup
of coffee and a little quiet time. The warmth of the sun, the songs
of birds nestled in the nearby tree, and the gentle breezes all invited
me to stay awhile and savor a beautiful spring afternoon. I began
to reflect on the freshness of the season—a time of transitions and
new beginnings. My mind soon shifted focus to this season of my
life—a season filled with transitions and new beginnings for myself
and for each member of my family.

As I thought about the many changes that have occurred in
our lives during the past few years, one stood out clearly to me
on that quiet afternoon. The bird's nest in my nearby tree held
little ones, but my nest is now empty. My children are now living
in their own places and establishing their lives as adults. I am
adjusting to the reality that they are not always available when

I want to talk or when I want them to come by for a visit. I've learned it's often best to leave text messages and extend invitations. I know they'll follow up when they can, sometimes with "Let's do it" and sometimes with "Let's make it another time." And the visits we share seem to go by all too quickly. In fact, earlier that very afternoon I commented to my husband (okay, maybe I whined a bit?) that I had not seen one of our sons in a while.

"He doesn't come over as much as I thought he would when he moved out," I lamented. "I've tried to invite him for dinner the past few days, but I can't seem to catch up with him."

"He's busy working and taking care of himself," my husband quickly responded, "which is a good thing, don't you agree?"

"I know, I know. I just thought we'd see him more often." My words spoke about a schedule, but I think my heart was struggling at that moment for reassurance that we were not losing connection with him. Then I had flashbacks of times we would visit our parents, all of whom lived out of town. No matter how often we went or how long we stayed, both mothers always said the visits were too short and too long in between.

Oh, no, I thought to myself, *I'm sounding just like them!*

"He comes when he can, and he knows he's always welcome," my husband reminded me. Perhaps he was trying to assure me that while our family time together has shifted to accommodate the changes taking place for all of us, we are still firmly connected, and our children know they are always welcome.

Interestingly, as I sat on the porch giving myself a pep talk, remembering that we have a loving relationship with our son and we were merely adjusting to a new aspect of our connection together, I looked up to see him walk in the front door.

"Hi," he greeted. "I thought I'd drop by before heading to work. I've been so busy and haven't had a chance to catch up. How are y'all?"

"Great," I replied with a smile on my face and a quiet sigh of relief as I caught an amusing I-told-you-so glance from my husband.

We talked for a bit and then he headed for the door. "I've got to run. Sorry I can't stay to eat. Maybe another time. I'll see you soon. Love you both."

I finished my coffee as my husband's words of assurance settled my mind and assured my heart: *"He knows he's always welcome."*

As parents of adult children, our task now is to find ways to communicate to our children that the welcome mat is out and there's a place for them in our homes and in our hearts. We've talked in earlier chapters about the need to respect their autonomy and learn how to work with them to meet their needs and desires as well as our own. So we must let them know the door is open, and place a welcome mat out that is inviting and not cluttered with demands, pressure, guilt, or threats of punishment.

> Our children need to know that no matter what road they travel, there's a path that leads to home and there's a welcome mat out for them.

We've also discussed the need to set and maintain healthy boundaries with our children. So as we extend that open invitation, we need to communicate the expectations we have for those who enter our home and what they can expect from us in return. When we share open communication, respect for each other's needs and schedules, and clear understanding, we can then relax and enjoy time together.

Extending a welcome to our children begins in our hearts and then extends to our front doors. That means we may have to let go of hurts and disappointments. We may have to be ready with forgiveness and grace. And we may have to leave the porch light on so the welcome mat is visible from afar as we develop patience to watch, pray, hope, and wait on them to come when they are ready.

Early this morning I was barely up and moving when I heard a knock at the front door. I glanced out the window and saw my neighbor, so I hurried to answer. We talked briefly and then she left. As I closed the door, my first thought was one of regret that I wasn't ready for her visit. But then I relaxed with a feeling of satisfaction that she knew she was welcome to come at any time. It wasn't about how I was dressed or if the house was ready for guests; it was a matter of a friend needing help from another friend and trusting the door would be open. She believed she would be welcome. And she was.

Our children need to know that when they need us, the welcome mat is out and woven with threads of understanding.

My husband got an unexpected call from an old friend recently. He and his wife were traveling in our area and wanted to stop by our home. We had not seen each other in quite some time, so the thought of reconnecting with them was great. I would have preferred to meet another day when I could have had more time to plan and prepare, but I knew I needed to be flexible. So we juggled our schedules a bit and found a way to share an enjoyable evening together. We were glad they felt welcome to come by.

Our children need to know that we want to share time with them, whether planned celebrations or simply relaxation and fun together, and we will work with them to find opportunities to do so. Let your welcome mat be woven with threads of desire and flexibility.

We celebrated Easter this spring with our sons, our daughter-in-law, and our new little granddaughter. We were so excited to have them all come to our home and share the holiday as a family. My husband prepared a scrumptious meal, and I made sure all was set with special touches to honor the day and the time together. As soon as we caught a glimpse of their cars, we hurried out to meet them. The welcome mat was shimmering with excitement and anticipation. Its greeting was far-reaching.

Our children need to know that time with them is of value to us. We can reach out with excitement to let them know they are special. Let your welcome mat be woven with threads of joy.

I have a friend who talks about coming to visit me. I've extended the invitation often but she has yet to follow through. I think she's dealing with some life issues and closing herself off from those who care about her. I can't go get her and make her come, nor do I want to shut the door. So I've determined the best I can do is leave the welcome mat out and hope someday she will come. She knows that while I may not agree with her on some matters, I love her, respect her choices, and will always have a place for her in my home and heart.

Our children need to know that no matter what road they travel, there's a path that leads to home and there's a welcome mat out for them. Let it sit on a foundation of love and be woven with God's principles for life and His desires for family. And let the porch light of hope shine bright to lead the way.

On a Personal Note

How do you communicate to your children that the welcome mat is out? With words? Actions?

Is your welcome mat woven with threads of understanding? Desire? Joy? Flexibility? Grace?

Is the light of hope shining bright so they can find their way if they wander off?

Take steps today to make certain the welcome mat for your home and your heart is one that will draw your children close and allow them to see God's love at work in the life of your family. And let the light of His love shine bright.

The Next Chapter

We've taken a look at the changes, challenges, and choices our children are experiencing now that they are adults. And we've looked at how our lives are changing, bringing our own challenges and choices. As we've shared these thoughts together, we've uncovered secrets to help us lovingly and effectively support our adult children while also caring for ourselves. We've heard words of insight and words of encouragement, we've paused to take our own personal inventory, and we've challenged ourselves to take steps to sharpen our parenting skills and improve our own lives in the process. And yet . . .

There are more experiences, more challenges, more lessons to learn, and more secrets to share as we travel this parenting journey. So I'll close with this word of encouragement: Let's take time to reflect on whatever life brings our way, and ask God to open the eyes of our minds and hearts and to guide our steps. And let's step out with confidence as we anticipate all that's in store for us and for our families. Then let's share our words of insight and encouragement—the *secrets* that help us nurture our relationships and experience life to the fullest.

I can't wait to see where this parenting journey will take us. . . . I hope I'll meet you along the way!

Notes

Introduction: Just When You Thought Your Work Was Done . . .

1. Stephen A. Bly, *Once a Parent Always a Parent: How to Love and Support Your Adult Children* (Wheaton, IL: Tyndale House, 1993), 25.

Chapter 1: Step One: Know What You're Getting Into

1. Lois Lieberman Davitz, PhD, and Joel R. Davitz, PhD, *Getting Along (Almost) With Your Adult Kids: A Decade-by-Decade Guide* (Notre Dame, IN: Sorin Books, 2003), 15–16.
2. Jane Adams, PhD, *When Our Grown Kids Disappoint Us* (New York: Free Press, Simon & Schuster, 2003), 3.

Chapter 2: Be Their Coach Without Taking Charge

1. L. Cecile Adams, "Characteristics of an Effective Spiritual Coach," in *Coaching by the Book* by Ruth Ledesma, with members of the Christian Coaches Network (Xlibris Corp., 2001), Appendix A.

Chapter 3: Create a Fresh Start

1. Jane Adams, 149.
2. Stephen A. Bly, 196.
3. Choleric personalities tend to be strong-willed, bold, dynamic, goal-oriented, and decisive. They can also appear impatient, inflexible, controlling, and sometimes even rude toward others.

Chapter 4: Set Healthy Boundaries—and Follow Through

1. Allison Bottke, *Setting Boundaries With Your Adult Children: Six Steps to Hope and Healing for Struggling Parents* (Eugene, OR: Harvest House, 2008), 33.
2. Dr. Henry Cloud and Dr. John Townsend, *Boundaries: When to Say Yes and When to Say No to Take Control of Your Life* (Grand Rapids, MI: Zondervan, 1992), 85.

Chapter 5: Handle Disappointments With Care

1. Jane Adams, 155.

Chapter 7: Bring Your Children Before the Lord

1. Stormie Omartian, *The Power of Praying for Your Adult Children* (Eugene, OR: Harvest House, 2009), 3.
2. Kitti Murray, *A Long Way Off* (Nashville: Broadman & Holman, 2004), 62.

Chapter 9: Give Yourself Some TLC

1. Janice Hanna and Kathleen Y'Barbo, *The House Is Quiet, Now What?* (Uhrichsville, OH: Barbour, 2009), 40–41.

Chapter 11: Offer Resources—When the Door Is Open

1. Taken from *www.AskPatty.com*, and used with permission.

About the Author

Nancy Williams is a licensed professional counselor and has received training as a life coach from the Institute of Life Coach Training—Christian Track. She has a BS degree in social studies from the University of Mary Hardin-Baylor, and a master's degree in counseling and human development from Lamar University.

Nancy maintains a counseling, coaching, and consulting practice where she works with adults in a Christian setting on a variety of life management issues. She enjoys frequent opportunities to speak and writes an inspirational column for community newspapers in the northeast Houston, Texas area. She is a member of First Baptist Church, Wimberley.

Nancy has been married thirty-six years, is the mother of two adult sons and a daughter-in-law, and is a proud new grandmother.